Obama Senior

A Dream Fulfilled

Kenway Autobiographies

Obama Senior

A Dream Fulfilled

Fredrick Donde

Kenway Publications

Nairobi • Kampala • Dar es Salaam • Kigali • Lilongwe •Lusaka

Published by
Kenway
an imprint of
East African Educational Publishers Ltd.
Brick Court, Mpaka Road/Woodvale Grove Westlands,
P. O. Box 45314, Nairobi – 00100, KENYA
Tel: +254 20 2324762 / 2324757 / 2324760
Cell: +254 722 205 660 / 733 677 716 / 722 207 216
Email: eaep@eastafricanpublishers.com
Website: www.eastafricanpublishers.com

East African Educational Publishers also has offices or is represented in the following countries: Uganda,
Tanzania, Rwanda, Malawi, Zambia, Botswana, Namibia and South Sudan.

ISBN: 978-9966-56-039-1

Printed in Kenya by
Printwell Industries Ltd.
P.O. Box 5216-0506
Nairobi, Kenya

CONTENTS

I have cherished the ideal of a democratic and free society in which all persons live together in harmony and with equal opportunities. It is an ideal which I hope to live for and to achieve. But if need be, it is an ideal for which I am prepared to die.

— Nelson Mandela, 1964

To

My parents, Esau and Eva
You are the love and light within us.

My wife, Mary
My companion in life, sadly missed, warmly remembered.
Your spirit lives on!

And to

All *jo-dak* (immigrants)
Frowned upon by others of a better claim, your lot is often precarious.
Yet, we are all sojourners in this mysterious journey of life.

Foreword

Iwas a young man growing up when I first 'met' my cousin, Barack Hussein Obama Senior in Ka'Rachuonyo at K'Obama Village in Southern Nyanza, Kenya. Their family lived in Nyang'oma K'Ogelo in Siaya County in Central Nyanza, but he was a regular visitor to Ka'Rachuonyo, where he was born and spent most of his early years before his father, Hussein Obama Onyango, migrated to Alego. I had no inkling that he was destined for greater things. All I noted was a serious and stern-looking individual who brooked no dissent. But maybe that was because I was still young, and I was yet to know him.

When, later in 1966, he invited me to live with him at his family house in Woodley Estate in Nairobi, I had just joined high school. I was to stay with him until I finished my secondary-level education four years later. As I got to know him better, I was exposed fully to his generous heart and his frank and honest opinion on a broad range of issues. I experienced first-hand his fearlessness that sometimes bordered on insolence, and his happy-go-lucky side. I was much younger than him, but we had become buddies.

He was always free and uninhibited with me, and that is how I first heard him speak proudly of his children – and about his son in a faraway land. I was to hear much more about him. We had a fine time together, and I was witness to the highs and lows in the life of Barack Obama Senior. We enjoyed the good life together at Woodley Estate. That was when he worked for the Ministry of Economic Planning, and though the job had its share of frustrations, the income was good, allowing him to lead a respectable life. Yes, the politics affected him, too. The undercurrents were always there, the simmering tensions between the independence leaders. Corruption had already reared its ugly head too, and listening to street talk and murmured conversations among the townspeople, one could not fail to notice the build up to a confrontation of some sort.

I was in Nairobi that fateful afternoon of 5 July 1969, when Tom Mboya, then Minister for Economic Planning, was felled by a lone gunman in the dusty streets of Nairobi. I can never forget that date. For, as if on cue, the entire nation rose up in anger and riots, with angry mobs running amok in the streets and threatening the very fabric of the young nation. Many things happened in the aftermath of that terrible deed, but whatever can be said, Kenya was never the same again.

And so was my friend, Barack Obama Senior. Indeed, he had become more than just a cousin; we were true friends who shared in the ebb and flow of life, and who had witnessed some of the most important events and periods of each other's lives. Following Tom Mboya's assassination, and the unfolding socio-economic and political environment, he lost his customary confidence and verve for life. Soon, an uncharacteristic furtiveness crept in, and he hit the bottle harder. Yes, there was talk of threats to his life, of strange cars trailing him in the night, and of near-misses on the road.

By that time, he had helped me get my first job in the Coca Cola Company's Nairobi Bottlers' plant in 1971, where I would serve until my retirement 25 years later. I was there when he lost his job at the Ministry, and when the worst happened – when he was unceremoniously bundled out of his house at Woodley. It was my turn to offer refuge, and I hosted him at my humble quarters in New Ngara Flats on the other side of town. That was probably the lowest point of his life, and he became greatly disillusioned. Still, he kept himself useful, helping with administrative duties at Chandlane Nursing Home in Nairobi that was owned by his old friend, Dr Oluoch.

When news of his death reached us that morning of 2 November 1982, the entire Obama Opiyo family was devastated. From Alego K'Ogelo in Siaya to Ka'Rachuonyo in the shores of Lake Victoria, wailing rent the air. Just as he had lost both a friend and mentor with the death of Tom Mboya, it was now my turn to experience that tragic loss. Not much could be said about the circumstances of his death, but a number of rather strange road accident deaths of prominent personalities in Kenya were to become the vogue around the same time.

From the lowest of lows at his tragic death, I have lived to see the great transformation that has occurred. I was on hand to meet Barack Obama on his first visit to Kenya in 1986, when I hosted him for dinner in my house. When he again visited Kenya with Michelle in 1992, they spent a night in my mother's house in K'Obama Village in Kendu Bay. He later invited me to his inauguration as Senator of Illinois in Washington, DC, on 4 January 2005. We met again when he came back as a US Senator in 2008, and I was present alongside other family members at his inauguration as the 44th president of the USA on 20 January 2009.

As for Barack Obama Snr, many people only know the public face, his suave, eloquent and rather brusque manner. Not many know the other side of my late friend and cousin, what I prefer to call his 'real' self. He had dreams, great dreams for his country and for himself. He exerted himself in pursuit of that dream, and in that process may have stepped on some powerful toes in the corridors of power. Yes, he made mistakes, and his domestic life was at times quite complex and convoluted, but he had a way of negotiating those challenges and paradoxes. A pioneers' life is lonely, and he did not have many people to look up to in his environment. In his search for personal meaning, he may have made mistakes that affected his career and working life and that may have contributed to his early demise.

As somebody who witnessed him wage that struggle courageously and with tenacity, I have nothing but the deepest respect for Barack Obama Snr. I have seen some uncannily familiar traits in his son the President, and I am glad that the latter seems to have learnt from the mistakes of the former, and avoided the pitfalls that so effectively stymied the life of an honest and potentially great man and leader.

It is my sincere hope that this book may help in some way in bringing to light the little known side of Barack Obama Snr, and of the complex circumstances that attended his life, including the fine balancing act that he was constantly called upon to perform.

Ezra Obama
June 2015

Preface

"Every man is trying to either live up to his father's expectations or make up for his father's mistakes."
– President Barack Obama, 2004

The father figure is central to a child's life and upbringing and Barack Obama must have felt deeply saddened by the death of his father that fateful day in November 1982 as a teenager. Though he wrote the above quote as an adult, his grandfather Hussein Onyango Obama since long gone, is quoted to have made a rather prophetic statement around 1940, when Obama Snr his father, was still a toddler. Relatives quote him as having said: "My name will be great; it will be written in many newspapers and read about all over the world." And so it became, through his progeny Obama Snr and his grandson President Barack Obama.

When Barack Obama, then a Senator of the US state of Illinois, visited his father's home country Kenya in 2006, and in particular the village in Nyang'oma K'Ogelo, Siaya County, I was privileged to be present at that meeting. During his speech on that occasion, he said that he was impressed that his father had come from such depths of poverty and with the support of the community, made it to Harvard University – one of America's most prestigious institutions of higher learning.

The following day, I was also honoured to be part of the UNICEF team that hosted Michelle Obama during her visit to a street children's rehabilitation centre at Kayole in Nairobi, where she gave a moving and strangely personal speech, telling the children that despite their poverty-stricken backgrounds, they could still make it big in life. At that time, he had not declared his candidacy, but those two speeches left me fully convinced that Barack Obama would run for the US presidency. I was therefore scarcely surprised by Obama's announcement to run for the top seat. I had seen it coming. What I found more surprising was the general feeling of doubt that greeted it. He had done his groundwork well, however, and had anticipated the reaction: "I recognise there is a certain presumptuousness in this – a certain audacity – to this announcement," he said. "I know that I haven't spent a lot of time learning the ways of Washington. But I've been there long enough to know that the ways of Washington must change."

My decision to write this book was therefore by chance rather than by choice. My interest was driven by the fact that Obama Snr and I hailed from the same region of Kenya. Also, his extended family and mine were well versed with each other. Of course, at the time, nobody dared imagine the unimaginable – that his son would win the US presidency. After some serious soul searching, I made the decision. I had not authored a book before and thus entertained some doubts, but I remembered both Barack's and Michelle's speeches in Kenya. If Barack Obama found it achievable to run for the presidency of the US, why on earth did I think writing a book impossible? I decided to write the story myself. I put pen to paper and commenced the work. This book is the result.

Fredrick Donde
Nairobi, June 2015

Acknowledgements

I take this early opportunity to acknowledge the support and cooperation of the following people without whom the work would not have been possible. First and foremost, I am greatly indebted to Mama Sarah, the indefatigable maternal grandmother of the President, who gave the go-ahead for the story of her 'son' to be written. As the family's focal point, she has proved a willing and invaluable source of information. I must also thank Peter Oloo Aringo, former Minister of Education and MP for Alego-Usonga Constituency, and Joe Donde, formerly MP for Gem Constituency, who together helped me get Mama Sarah's blessing and cooperation for the project, and who subsequently opened many a door for me through their contacts, near and far.

I would also like to appreciate the help and facilitation of the following individuals with whom we interacted for their support: Ezra Obama, Mwana Hawa Auma Magak, Elijah K'Obilo, Wilson Obama, Amir Otieno Orinda, Razik Salmin Madoro, Zarifa Akello Miragi, Francis Ngesa, Prof Terry Ryan, Patrick Obath, Jack Okeyo, Jerry Owuor, Milka Ondiek, John Okeyo, Jared Onono, Caleb Omogi, Simeon Ochieng', Francis Masakhalia, Moses Wasonga, Nick Ajuoga, Prof Peter Kenya, Mary Odinga, Mzee James Odalo, Rev David Otieno, Betty Odhiambo, Alice Majuma, Francis Mayaka, and Francis Oling'a; Phoebe Asiyo, Janet Onyango, Jarawila Ajwang', Mzee Tago, Vincent Matinde, Paul Onyango 'Maji', Juddy Opiyo; Joseph Adero Ngala, Steve Ouma, Fr Joakim Omolo, Fr Cornway (MM), Wycliff Nyakina, Alloyce Ojore and Adonijah Nyamwanda.

I also wish to appreciate Bishop David Oyedepo, General Overseer of Winner's Chapel, for his inspirational influence. My special acknowledgements to Julius Opiyo and Joe Donde for the labour of love, tracing out people – friends, distant relations, extracting sometimes painful memories and stories from them. For the researchers Julius Opiyo, Amos B Omollo, Francine Buna, and Hillary Ang'awa – thank you very much too for your effort. I wish to thank Henry Chakava of East African Educational Publishers and Phoebe Mugo of Uzima Publishing House for their great encouragement and astute publishing insights.

I am also greatly indebted to my editor and project manager, Amos B Omollo. Your skills and talents have been one of my greatest assets, helping fashion a story from the complex maze of information, sifting through it all with a fine toothcomb. Without you, there would be no story.

Other people also contributed either directly or indirectly to this project. Since it may not be possible to acknowledge you all by name, please accept this as my sincere appreciation for your role. Finally, I wish to register my deep appreciation for my immediate family members who faithfully stood by me during the course of writing this story.

Note
President Barack Obama has been consistently referred to as President even when he was not, just to differentiate him from his father, Barack Obama Senior.

Abbreviations

AASF	–	African-American Student Foundation
ACOA	–	American Committee on Africa
CBK	–	Central Bank of Kenya
CMS	–	Christian Missionary Society
DRC	–	Democratic Republic of the Congo
ICA	–	International Cooperation Administration
EEC	–	European Economic Community
IIE	–	Institute of International Education
KANU	–	Kenya African National Union
KAR	–	King's African Rifles
KBC	–	Kenya Broadcasting Corporation
KTDC	–	Kenya Tourism Development Corporation
NPCP	–	Nairobi People's Convention Party
ODM	–	Orange Democratic Movement
UNHCR	–	United Nations High Commissioner for Refugees
UNICEF	–	United Nations Children's Fund
USA	–	United States of America
YMCA	–	Young Men's Christian Association

The family tree

OPIYO

1. *Nyar* Nyakach 2. *Nyar* Mbita Wasaki

Obama Opiyo

1.	2.	3.	4.
Augo *Nyar* Mwala	**Nyaoke**	**Omwanda *Nyar* Aketch** ***Nyar* Aketch**	**Odero**

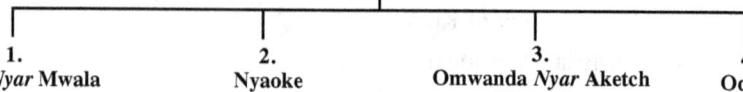

1. Child deserted
Onyango Hussein Obama
Augo Salmon Oguta Obama
Patrick Ojwang Obama
Jonathan Ndako Obama

2. Ndalo Okingo obama
Joshua Ogembo Obama
Susan Opiyo
Wilkitsa Ocholla

1. Zakayo Obilo Obama
Drusila Akoth

1. Rebecca Obongo Aura

5.
Auma

Blasto Adhiambo
Auma Origa
Dulo
Apiyo
Adongo

Hussein Onyango Obama

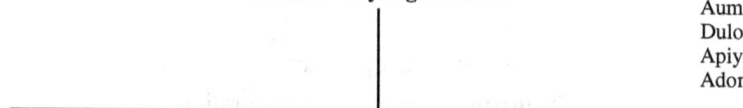

1.	2.	3.
Halima	**Habiba Akumu *nyar* Njoga**	**Sarah Ogwel**
No children		Obama Onyango
(ran away)		Zeituni Abong'o

Sarah
Obama Snr
Hawa Auma
Amir
Razik

Yusuf Hussein
Marfat Osumba
Ojijo

Barack Hussein Obama Snr
1936–1982

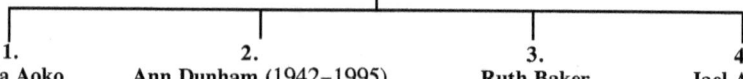

1.	2.	3.	4.
Kezia Aoko	**Ann Dunham (1942–1995)**	**Ruth Baker**	**Jael Atieno**
Roy Malik Abong'o	President Barack Hussein Obama	Mark Okoth	George Onyango
Rita Auma	Maya Soetoro (1970)	David Opiyo	Melvin
Samson Nyandega			Christine
Bernard Otieno			

Barack Hussein Obama (1961)

Michelle Obama (1964)

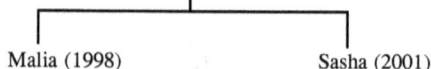

Malia (1998)   Sasha (2001)

The six nations in Eastern Africa where the Luo-speaking people live

Africa

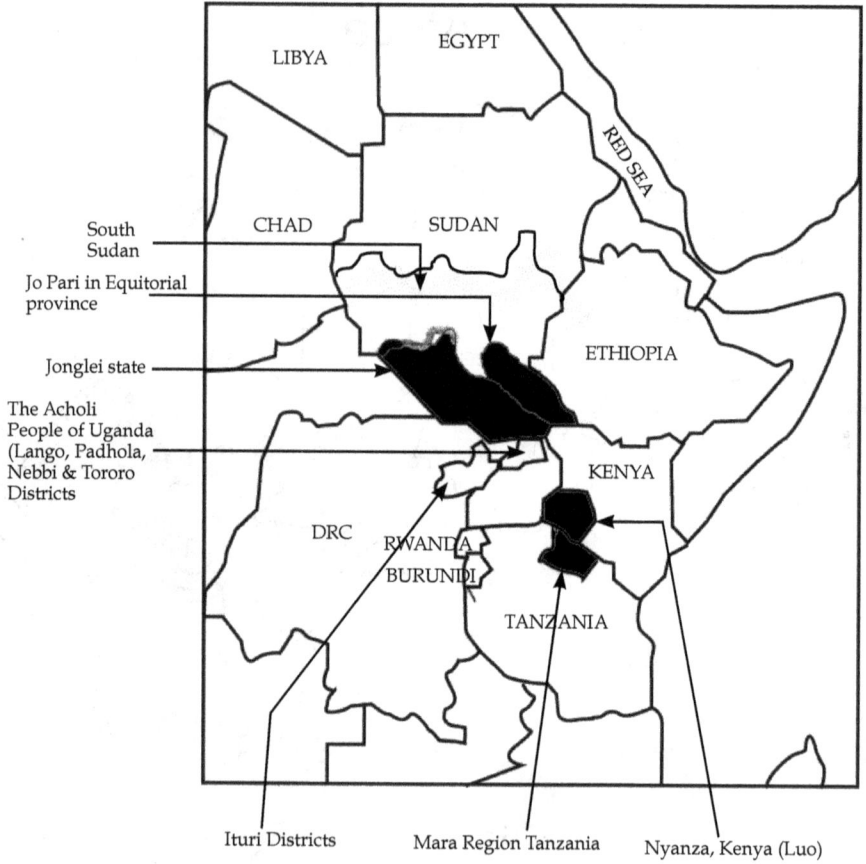

LIBYA

EGYPT

RED SEA

South Sudan

Jo Pari in Equitorial province

CHAD

SUDAN

ETHIOPIA

Jonglei state

The Acholi People of Uganda (Lango, Padhola, Nebbi & Tororo Districts

KENYA

DRC

RWANDA

BURUNDI

TANZANIA

Ituri Districts

Mara Region Tanzania

Nyanza, Kenya (Luo)

Chapter 1

Jo'Kogelo, the Forebears

K'Ogelo onge nyieke
(A Luo saying meaning 'The K'Ogelo have no co-wife')

Obama Snr belongs to the *K'Ogelo* (descendants of Ogelo), which is one of the sub-clans of the larger Alego Clan. The Alego are among the more than two dozen clans of the Luo, which is one of Kenya's 42 ethnic groups. Nyang'oma K'Ogelo in Alego, located in Central Nyanza on the northern side of Lake Victoria in Siaya County, was the JoK'Obama (descendants of Obama) original home in Kenya. Ng'iya is a significant market centre in the locality. The parliamentary constituency is known as Alego-Usonga. Initially described by many international journalists as a sleepy village, Nyang'oma K'Ogelo nevertheless turned tables and became a household name as the 2008 US presidential campaigns gathered momentum.

While Obama Snr hailed from the Alego Clan in Siaya County, his great-grandfather had migrated more than a hundred years before he was born to the present-day Rachuonyo Sub-County located in Homa Bay County. That is where the majority of his relatives still live today. This second group of the Obama relatives are part of the migrant K'Ogelo people in K'Obama Village, Ka'Nyadhiang Sub-Location. In this second habitation, the K'Ogelo live among a major clan known as 'Ka'Rachuonyo'. In this locality, both the clan and the parliamentary constituency carry the name 'Ka'Rachuonyo'.

Historically, having migrated from South Sudan through Uganda, the Luo first arrived in Kenya in the period 1490-1517 in three main

1

successive waves comprised of the Joka-Jok, Jok'Owiny and Jok'Omolo. The first wave of Joka-Jok settlers were led by one Ramogi Ajwang, who became the first Luo to arrive in Kenya.[1] He settled at a place known as *Got Ramogi* (Ramogi Hill) on the shores of Lake Victoria. Today, the Kenya Luo identify themselves as *nyikwa* (offsprings of) Ramogi Ajwang.[2] *Got Ramogi* is now a national monument registered with the National Museums of Kenya.

The second wave of Luo migration comprised the Jok'Owiny led by Owiny, who moved to Kenya from Uganda after parting ways with his brother, Adhola – the progenitor of the Jo'Padhola of Uganda. The Jok'Owiny were divided into three distinct groups. From their dispersal point at Pakwach or Pubungu in the present-day Uganda, one group came directly to Kenya. The second group – the Adhola cluster – came to Kenya via Busoga, while the third group, the Joka'Ruoth (royal clan) came to Kenya via Budoola. The K'Ogelo, and by extension the Obamas, belong to the Ka'Ruoth cluster of the Jok'Owiny.

Among the descendants of Owiny was a man known as Kisodhi, who eventually settled with his family near what is today the Uranga township in Siaya County. His eldest son was known as Ogelo.[3] According to tradition, Ogelo eventually moved out of his father's homestead and settled in the place that is presently known as Ng'iya in Alego, Siaya County. This area became known as K'Ogelo (the home or place of Ogelo) after his name. Ogelo became the progenitor of the now famous Obama family. The third wave of the Joka' Omolo arrived from Uganda through Samia.

The early Luo migrations from Central Nyanza to South Nyanza were caused by several push and pull factors acting in tandem. The push factors included regular destruction of food crops and lives by wild animals, especially elephants and hippos, in the early Luo settlements in Central Nyanza.

---

[1] Bethwell Ogot (2009). *A History of the Luo-Speaking Peoples of Eastern Africa*, pp. 487–488.
[2] Samuel Ayany, *Kar Chakruok mar Luo* (*The Origins of the Luo*), p. 4.
[3] T Olunga Ayot, (1987) *Luo Settlement*, p. 110.

Others sought peace and refuge in the new lands to the south, away from slave raiders who captured and sold the people to Arab traders in exchange for beads and other treasures. People also migrated due to population increase – and also because the areas they occupied were no longer productive enough, exposing them to hunger and famine.

On the other hand, the Luo found the new lands in Ka'Rachuonyo verdant, and fish was abundantly available from the lake, assuring them of fresh supplies all year round.

According to available estimates, the migrations started in the period 1730–1790 and continued back and forth over many generations.[4] In those days, some parts of the lake were not as deep as it is today. According to legend, it was possible to walk right across the lake from Uyoma in Central Nyanza to Mirunda Bay in Ka'Rachuonyo, or from Asembo Bay to Ka'Rachuonyo. People generally migrated in large groups composed of people from the same clan, including their animals.

Each of the clans had their own leader or chief, together with a *ja-bilo* (seer-magician) who advised the chief on all significant events, especially those related to movement, diplomacy and war. Leadership was important for diplomacy and formation of alliances, but a powerful *ja-bilo* was essential to win a war, since it was only the *ja-bilo* who could foretell events, espy the enemy through remote viewing, and devise schemes to counter the plans of the enemy. The office of the *ja-bilo* – the seer-magician – was different from that of the *ja-thieth* or *ajuoga* – the medicine man or healer – but some people could combine the two functions, being both magicians and healers. In those days, it was critical to scout the land in advance, for the dangers were many and the journey unpredictable. Before the main body of the clan could move, special teams known as *ligawa* were sent ahead to scout the land. It was only after the reception of a favourable scouting report that the people were mobilised to undertake the journey.[5]

---

[4] T. Olunga Ayot (1987), *Luo Settlement in South Nyanza*.
[5] Gordon Wilson, *Luo Customary Law and Marriage Customs*, p.24.

The K'Ogelo Clan of the Obamas was one of the several that were involved in periodic settlements during the last two hundred years. Having migrated from Alego, the great-grandfather of Obama Snr, Opiyo, was one of the early settlers in Ka'Rachuonyo.

As with the rest of the Kenya Luo, the history of the K'Ogelo and *Jo*-Ka'Rachuonyo can be traced many years back. In legend, they trace their origins from a common ancestor, Ramogi, who lived around Ramogi Hill in Central Nyanza. One of his sons was named Jok. He and his wife Awandu had four sons – Chwanya, Nyasgenga, Omwa and Rachuonyo. The Ka'Rachuonyo Clan traces its ancestry to the last born son of Jok, Rachuonyo. The folk history of the dispersal goes as follows.

While still at their Ramogi Hill settlement, the Luo had started practicing agriculture. Wild animals, especially elephants and hippopotamus, freely roamed the land, destroying crops in their wake. It was thus customary to guard the fields, more so at night. One day, the story goes, Jok was invited to a beer party at a friend's home. He asked his sons to go and guard the fields in the night since he intended to stay late. They all refused.

After their father had gone, the children had second thoughts and eventually decided to keep an eye on the fields. The old man too decided to pass by and check the crops on his way back. Doubtless terrified by the unrelenting wilderness, one of his sons, scared witless by blundering noises coming from the bushes, and thinking that it might be an elephant or hippo marauding on the farm, threw a spear. It impaled the old man through, and he fell prostrate, groaning and lamenting that his sons had killed him.

Horrified, the sons scattered in the darkness. In the tradition of the Ka'Rachuonyo, the name of the son who killed him is given as Nyasgenga. Ka'Rachuonyo tradition reports that he was cursed and disappeared completely. He went into exile among the neighbouring Bantu people, the Abagusii. There he multiplied and waxed great. His descendants became very numerous, and in time grew into what today is known as the Wanjare Clan of the Abagusii.

Rachuonyo, who also disappeared at the time of his father's death, is said to have run and hid in between the papyrus reeds along the shores of the lake – at a place referred to as Gangu or *Nam Bonya*. He was later found by three old men – Nyakwar, Ogelo and Chien. It is from this Ogelo that the K'Ogelo Clan, and by extension, the Obama family, descended. This early relationship between the K'Ogelo and Ka'Rachuonyo would explain why, in later years, the K'Ogelo found it convenient to settle among the Ka'Rachuonyo.

Rachuonyo subsequently became the proud owner of a dog known as Sipul, who helped him become an expert hunter. Man and beast became so close such that, in later years, he named one of his sons after his favourite dog. He later migrated and settled in South Nyanza in the area which came to be known as Ka'Rachuonyo. He was one of the earliest Luo people to settle in the area. In the present-day Kenya, Rachuonyo Sub-County is named after Rachuonyo. Ka'Rachuonyo is the largest single unit occupied by the Luo in South Nyanza. There are also parliamentary constituencies named after both Rachuonyo and his son Sipul where their descendants live. These are Ka'Rachuonyo and Ka'Sipul-Ka'Bondo constituencies.

* * *

As has already been mentioned, the K'Ogelo had a longstanding relationship with the Ka'Rachuonyo. On the other hand, Rachuonyo, the progenitor of the Ka'Rachuonyo, had a brother named Chwanya who in turn had a son called Onyango Rabala. At one moment, Chwanya had been taken hostage to be sold as a misumba (slave) to slave traders. As was the custom, when one was taken by slave traders it was normal that he would never be seen again. In that case, he was presumed dead and traditional rites commenced in his honour.

It was the brave act of one of his sons, Onyango, which rescued Chwanya. Gathering courage, he braved all dangers and pursued his father's assailants unaided. In a typical David verses Goliath struggle, he fought them off and brought his father back. On his return, however, more trouble awaited. Nobody was prepared to perform the cleansing ritual that tradition decreed on somebody returning from the land of the dead. Calling upon his reserves again, Onyango did what had never been imagined before – he performed the ritual himself. In appreciation, his father gave him the honourable title, *Rabala*, the indefatigable one.

As a final honour, Chwanya poured all his blessings upon Onyango. Offering Onyango a spear and a hoe, he intoned: *"Tong'ni ineg godo le mangeny; kwer'ni ipur godo. Jogi enobedi mang'eny kendo gini go're kendgi. Mondi gini bedi Nyasgogo kaka meru."*("Take this spear; using it, you will become a great hunter. Take this hoe; a great farmer you shall be. Your descendants shall be multiplied, and they shall contend among themselves. Your women, they shall be unfaithful; they shall desert you just like your mother did to me.")

In resentment, his brothers ganged up against him and forced him into exile – to Rongo in South Nyanza. He eventually had many sons, among them Owiti, who was nicknamed *bwoch* (the eunuch) on account of his dull ways with the ladies. Still, Owiti eventually married, and his descendants became known as *Jo-ka-bwoch* ('people of the eunuch'), who became a force to reckon with. The descendants of Owiti multiplied greatly, had many livestock, and occupied large tracts of land.

The *Ka-bwoch* waxed great. Over the years, their numerical strength was captured in the proverbial saying, *uthoth ka K'Achieng Mawaganjo*. The saying is now rendered in its more common and simpler form, *utimo kachieng* – meaning 'you are as many as the *Ka-bwoch Kachieng'*. The *Ka-bwoch* who had settled in South Nyanza became embroiled in long running conflicts with *Jo-Lango* (the Maasai) for supremacy over the land. There was a lot of fighting in the area in the period 1825 AD–1850 AD.

In their quest to secure more productive land, the Luo Karungu and Kadem clans were among the earliest Luo settlers in the area now known as South Nyanza. Greatly outnumbered by their more numerous Bantu hosts, they faced great challenges at their beachhead in Sori. The Bantu made them perform all sorts of manual work and milk cows for them. They also felt obliged to take as wives nubile maidens from their Luo neighbours while the latter were only allowed to marry old and ugly women from them. That eventually led to a fight. According to Karungu tradition, the conflict flared during a joint hunting expedition between the two groups of warriors. In the heat of the chase at *Got* Bim, a rhino suddenly appeared from the bush and a Luo warrior, Owaha, speared it to death. It fell down struggling in a cloud of dust and breathed its last with its head facing Lake Victoria. That was construed as an omen for the Luo, who saw it as fulfillment of a prophecy, a sort of 'manifest destiny'. All the land from where they had settled right to the lake would be theirs, they reasoned. But the Bantu warriors had other ideas. The rhino horn must be delivered as tribute to their leader, Migowa, they demanded. The hunt had become a battle.

The Bantu warriors drew first blood – spearing one Olwalo K'Ochieng to death. Strangely, his death was received with much joy among his Luo compatriots. It had long been foretold in an ancient prophecy that the blood of a man would be shed for the land. *Olwalo K'Ochieng ne otho ne piny* (Owalo the son of Ochieng had shed his blood for the land); hence the land belonged to his people. The battle raged! It is here that the Luo started their dominance of the vast area now known as South Nyanza, including major locations in northern Tanzania, which eventually became Luo settlements.

The K'Ogelo settled in Ka'Rachuonyo over a period of several hundred years during the climax of the Luo migration from Central Nyanza to South Nyanza – which was originally occupied by diverse groups – among them the Maasai, Abagusii, Abakuria and several other groups with origins in Tanzania and Uganda. An account of the movement has been captured in the work of several historians, among them W R Ochieng,[6] Grace Ogot,[7] J M Lonsdale[8] and T Olunga Ayot.[9]

---

[6] W R Ochieng (1974). *Outline History of Nyanza*. Ochieng offers a detailed and thorough history not just of the Luo migration into South Nyanza, but much more.

[7] Grace Ogot (1966). *The Promised Land*. This is a fiction account, but rich in folklore.

[8] J M Lonsdale (1964). *A Political History of Nyanza, 1883–1954*. As the title suggests, this is a more academic rendition that covers the period of the migration as well as almost the entire colonial epoch.

[9] Ayot, T Olunga (1987). *Luo Settlement in South Nyanza*.

* * *

The journey taken by the K'Ogelo Clan from Alego to Ka'Rachuonyo in South Nyanza took several days. They first trekked from Alego to Yala, where they rested at the home of one Ogola *wuon* (son of) Ayieke. From there, their next stop was in the home of Joel Omono, in Ugenya. Moving southwards, the people went up to Got Agoro, thence through Nyahera in Kisumu County. Having crossed the River Nyando, they eventually rested in Nyakach.

Leaving Nyakach, they crossed the Sondu-Miriu River and entered Kabondo in South Nyanza, from where they eventually moved to the present Oyugis area. While some of the K'Ogelo settled in this area, others proceeded to Rangwe and rested at the home of one Obuogo *wuon* Njoge in Kamagambo. From Kamagambo, they went to Kitere, where they stayed for some time before establishing the Ranjira and Alego settlements. Majority of the K'Ogelo settled in the area that is presently known as Rachuonyo Sub-County.

The present-day Rachuonyo Sub-County is quite expansive, covering an area of about 2,400 square kilometres. The area consists of two types of people of Luo origin. The first and numerically dominant group are the *jo-piny* (*indigenes* – the owners of the land), who claim direct descent from Rachuonyo. The other group, composed of minority settlers, is referred to as *jo-dak* (*allogenes* – immigrants). These are people who came from other areas and were offered land by the indigenous people of Ka'Rachuonyo. Since they were immigrant settlers from their original home in Central Nyanza, the Obamas and the whole of the K'Ogelo in Ka'Rachuonyo belong to the latter category

The K'Ogelo had settled in several localities in South Nyanza where they were regarded as *jo-dak* (immigrants). The life of the *jo-dak* was always fraught with dangers, for the 'owners' of the land believed that *jo-dak* took away the 'blessings' or prosperity, which would otherwise be reserved for them. They also contended that, in spite of their inferior position, the *jo-dak* tended to be more successful and prosperous. The lot of the *jo-dak* was thus regular persecution and violent expulsion.

It is no wonder that, in the settlements in South Nyanza, many groups did not wish to be referred to as *jo-dak*. They well knew the sorry fate of *jo-dak* in many places.

Some of the K'Ogelo including Jok'Obama had occupied the area known as Ka'Rachuonyo, while another group of the K'Ogelo occupied the area known as Kamagambo in South Nyanza. Determined to secure for his people a land of their own, Adoma, leader of the K'Ogelo, went to see Gor Mahia, chief of the neighbouring Kanyamwa Clan, to ask for permission to settle there. He agreed to give the southern section of Kanyamwa to the K'Ogelo. Delighted, Adoma went back to bring gifts to Gor to show his gratitude. However, while he was away, Owino *nyar* (daughter of) Obonyo, Gor's *Mikayi* (elder wife) reported to the Kanyamwa elders that Gor was giving away their land to the K'Ogelo. The elders prevailed on Gor so that he changed his mind.

Being seen as *jo-dak*, the Obama ancestors were greatly hated and feared by the Kamagambo and their chief, Ngoje. At one time, Ngoje had a quarrel with some K'Ogelo clansmen during a night funeral vigil. In the process, one of them, Awoth, speared him in the stomach, but he did not die. From that day, the Kamagambo swore never to forgive the K'Ogelo and to expel them at the earliest opportunity.

Paying tribute to the singular bravery of the K'Ogelo men who dared attack him, Ngoje, chief of the Kamagambo, remarked that, *kuodi K'Ogelo ok chwo tuchi,* literally meaning that 'no spears could penetrate the shields of the K'Ogelo'. In a real sense, what the chief meant was that, if the Obama ancestors were so brave as to attack the chief of the Kamagambo himself, then they were ready to challenge anybody.

Therefore Ngoje summoned all his people and they agreed as one to expel the K'Ogelo forthwith. They were to drive them to the River Kuja where they would all drown. Also known as River Gucha by the neighbouring Abagusii community, the River Kuja is infamous for the devastation it visits whenever it floods.

Chief Ngoje mobilised his people and made preparations to raze all the K'Ogelo homes. Luckily for Obama's ancestors, some K'Ogelo

9

girls had been married to the Kamagambo. The two prominent ones were Opiyo Nyareri and Mwalo *nyar* Ojwang'. The two women secretly warned the K'Ogelo not to sleep heavily as the Kamagambo planned to burn their homes. *"Ninduru ka ung'eyo ni kiny Kamagambo nowang'u; Ngoje ochoko ji nyaka mwalo ka' Mwango; kiny nowang'u gokinyi"*, they reported to their people. ('Sleep lightly knowing that tomorrow the Kamagambo will attack and burn down your homes; Chief Ngoje has mobilised his people as far as Mwango's; the attack will come in the morning.') When the K'Ogelo heard this, they called upon Nyariro, their leading musician to entertain them as they kept vigil through the night. Here at the dance place, the K'Ogelo planned their next move.

The following morning, Ngoje ordered his warriors to move to Kitere and raze the K'Ogelo homes. The Kamagambo chased them up to the mouth of the River Kuja, at a place known as Oringiti. Adoma and Rapemo, both expert *jo-bilo* (magicians) now led the K'Ogelo. At the bank of the raging River Kuja, the two leaders held age-old arcane ceremonies to divine the fate of the community and to determine how they would cross the river.

The Kamagambo believed that the river was impassable; they watched from afar, confidently expecting the Obama ancestors to drown *en masse* and stood guard to make sure that they would not retreat. But the K'Ogelo were determined to reach their 'promised land'. Much to the disappointment of the Kamagambo, the K'Ogelo magicians divined a new kind of craft, which their artisans quickly improvised. Soon, the river crossing began. The first four men to cross were Osoyi, Okungu, Duta and Owenga Nyagola – all expert fishermen and excellent swimmers. The men then successfully transported the women, children and K'Ogelo property across the river.

According to Luo tradition, when a new home is erected, a fire must be lit. This is provided from the old fire by the uncle of the person building the home. For the Obama ancestors, the Kamagambo could not give them the old fire. Instead, the K'Ogelo produced the new fire by rubbing together two pieces of wood, *orembe* and *nyadema*.

This earned them the fame enshrined in the saying, *K'Ogelo onge nyieke* (literally, the K'Ogelo have no co-wife or contender), meaning they were all alone and did not share their problems with any other group. Among the first livestock to make the crossing of the river were one special bull, *rwath larapinta,* and a cow belonging to Amuom *ja-*K'Ogelo. This cow was referred to as *jalim K'Ogelo* (the visitor of K'Ogelo) because it had visited all the K'Ogelo homes the night before they left Kamagambo. It was their ritual cow or *dher bilo.*

The confrontation took place at the turn of the century when the colonialists had already appointed the white administration, headed at the local level by a District Commissioner (DC). The following day, the Kamagambo sent an emissary to Kisii to report to the DC, Mr Campbell, that the K'Ogelo who lived at Kitere had been expelled and may have drowned in the swollen waters of the River Kuja. The DC and his interpreter, Jakasera, went out to investigate. Chief Ngoje of the Kamagambo explained to him why he had dislodged the K'Ogelo, adding that he did not wish to have them back for they were a threat to his people. He also contended that he did not want to see Adoma again since he had helped the K'Ogelo cross the river and gone to Aram *piny Lango* (that is, Aram land of the Maasai).

When Ongoro, who lived with his people in the land now bordered by the K'Ogelo, complained to the DC about the invasion, the DC prevailed upon him, saying that since the land was heavily forested and full of dangerous wild animals, it was perhaps to his advantage having the K'Ogelo as neighbours. Adoma and Ongoro agreed and embraced each other to show that they would live together as brothers. That meeting was held in 1912. Its original venue is presently the site of a bus stop at Raruowa near the home of one *Mzee* (elder) Midiwo.

In 1914, Ouma, an elder of K'Ogelo and a relative of Ondiek and Osawa died in Ka'Rachuonyo. As was expected, Ondiek and Osawa went for the funeral ceremony. They carried their spears and shields and, as they entered the home, they chanted war songs and performed ritualised war dances, as was customary among the Luo when a respected man

11

died. This was the great *tero buru* ritual, which is still practiced today among some sections of the community. However, since the Great War (World War I) was then raging, the colonial government forbade people to carry weapons. Sadly for them, Ondiek and Osawa had their shields burned. That was the year of *hik wang'o kuodi* (burning shields). Be that as it may, the K'Ogelo managed to get their own land in which to settle under the leadership of Adoma and Rapemo before the former's death at his home in 1925.

The settlement of the K'Ogelo in Aram explains the nature of what took place in South Nyanza. Once a leader had secured suitable land somewhere, he urged his people to come and settle, after which there would be much movement. Thus, the K'Ogelo became members of Aram and their settlements were situated around Got Rabuor on the northern end of Sakwa Kadera and Kanyamwa in present-day South Nyanza. The K'Ogelo who remained in Alego came to refer to the new home of the migrant K'Ogelo as Aram *piny* Adoma (Aram land of Adoma).

Chapter 2

The Obama Patriarchs

"You may call us mere settlers in Ka'Rachuonyo, men without substance and with no signs of obvious success. But mark my words! One day your name will fade into oblivion, but mine, my friend, mine will be read in books and newspapers across the world!"
 – Hussein Onyango Obama, 1938

A sizeable population of the K'Ogelo migrated from what is today Siaya County of Central Nyanza to Rachuonyo Sub-County in South Nyanza at the height of the Luo migration there. Among them was Opiyo, the great-grandfather of Barack Obama Snr who migrated to Rachuonyo Sub-County to join part of the now significant K'Ogelo community there. The patriarch, who grew up in Alego K'Ogelo, had a twin sister called Jalang'o who had got married to a man in Kanyadhiang', near Kendu Bay in Rachuonyo Sub-County, South Nyanza. "Due to her love for her twin brother," narrates Hezron Ogembo, a native of Kanyadhiang', "she invited him to join her in her matrimonial land." Thus it was that Opiyo migrated from Alego to Ka'Rachuonyo.

"He was a great man indeed," said Mama Sarah. Blessed with two wives and six children, he owned much land in Alego. When he left Alego, however, he had to start afresh in his new abode in Ka'Rachuonyo. All his herd of cattle had remained behind, and he was landless. Luckily for him, there was plenty of unused land, which tradition dictated could be utilised by any suitably disposed member of the community.

"In the custom of our people," explained Mama Sarah, "a man could utilise and lay claim to any unused land."

For the Luo, movement was engrained into their genetic makeup. When a boy came of age, he was first expected to move out of his parent's house and build his own hut (*simba*). Still later, he was expected to move out of his father's homestead altogether and erect his own home. The girls too were expected first to move to their grandmother's hut or the girls' dormitory (*siwindhe*), after which they were expected to find a suitable suitor and move out in marriage.

The Luo regarded the land as their mother, and the tribe as a whole was the proprietor of all the land within its jurisdiction. Within the tribe, clan or sub-clan, the individual laid claim to a piece of land or several pieces depending on his diligence, but he used the land for the benefit of his family only as long as he lived in the community; as soon as he left to live elsewhere the land reverted to the community and was allocated to the nearest neighbour or given to a newcomer joining the community. A parcel of land left uncultivated for a season could be used for grazing by anyone in the clan, without his having to seek permission or pay a fee. Strictly speaking, even cattle were not private but community property.

Opiyo, the great-great-grandfather of President Obama thus located suitable land that he cleared and claimed for himself. "By the time he moved from Alego to Ka'Rachuonyo, Opiyo had got married to two wives, one from Nyakach and the other from Mbita Wasaki, both in Nyanza. It was the latter that bore him his first born, a son that he named 'Obama'," Mama Sarah explains. Obama son of Opiyo was born in Ka'Rachuonyo.

Opiyo did not live long enough to prosper, however. He died early, leaving behind his widows and children, including Obama. As was the custom, his uncle took in one of the widows; she became his wife, her children his children. Unfortunately, his mother died soon thereafter, leaving him effectively orphaned while still a boy. "He, too, lived with his uncle, but the resources of the family were strained," adds Mama Sarah. And so, as Obama Opiyo grew older, "he began to work for other men as his father had done before him."

* * *

As soon as he came of age, Obama Opiyo started working, doing odd jobs for pay as was the custom among his people. He worked for a wealthy and well-disposed family who gradually recognised and admired him for his diligence and enterprise. When he sought to marry their eldest daughter, Augo *nyar* Mwala, they agreed, and his uncles provided the necessary dowry. She bore him a lovely baby girl, *nyar* Mwala, but she later left him after a family disagreement.

As a result, Obama Opiyo's sister, Mbidha, went to ask for another bride at Kanyadhiang', where Augo had come from. "Your daughter has left a toddler in our home," she explained to the in-laws. "Give us a girl to take care of her house." They obliged, providing her younger sister, Nyaoke, as replacement after recommendation by a relative, Achungo. The two were soon married.

When Nyaoke came to Obama's home, she was accompanied by her sister, Auma, who was highly skilled in the art of making *dero*, traditional Luo granaries for grain storage. He took a liking to her immediately. He consulted his wife, seeking her consent to marry her sister. Nyaoke agreed, and Auma became Obama Opiyo's third wife. Later on, he also got married to Odero and finally, Omwanda *nyar* Aketch.

Eventually, Obama Opiyo had five wives who bore him many children. He cleared his own land and became prosperous, with a large compound and many cattle and goats. According to Mama Sarah and other relatives, Obama Opiyo lived for a long time with his sons in Ka'Rachuonyo before leaving for Alego. Due to his industry and responsible ways, he became an elder in Kendu, and many came from far and wide to seek his advice.

When he left, he complained that he could not bear being called *ja-dak* by the people of Ka'Rachuonyo. He relocated to Alego with his family and established his own homestead. To their dismay, they found themselves in a land where food was scarce and famine rampant. This was in stark contrast to Ka'Rachuonyo that was a land of plenty. No matter how much he tried to be comfortable in Alego, it proved too difficult for him.

Finally, he decided that it was not a place where he could live.

"I am going back to my maternal parents' home," he decided. And so he left on the long journey back to Ka'Rachuonyo.

"It was one Orindo who convinced Obama K'Opiyo to make the move back to Ka'Rachuonyo from Alego," Elijah K'Obilo, a cousin of Obama Snr, takes up the story. According to K'Obilo, Obama K'Opiyo had eight sons. His first son, called Ndalo Obama, died in Alego. The second-born son was called Salmon Oluta Obama. Next was Hussein Onyango Obama, who became the father of Barack Obama Snr After Hussein was born Zakayo Obilo Obama, who in turn was followed by Joshua Ogendo Obama, who was followed by Blasto Odhiambo Obama. Next was Patrick Ojwang' Obama. The last born was named Ndalo Ochieng Obama after the first-born, Ndalo Obama, who had died.

All his life, Obama K'Opiyo was a non-conformist who had no qualms locking horns with tradition and breaking the rules when he felt that to do otherwise would be retrogressive. This trait he exhibited again and again. By challenging tradition, he helped his people see things in a different light. In that way, he was one of the pioneers of change.

Contrary to Luo customs and traditions of the time, Obama K'Opiyo gave his children equal treatment, boys and girls alike. Doubtless people protested, but he stubbornly insisted on gender equality for his progeny. Every girl and married woman was given a piece of land to plant crops and to fend for herself and her children. "Obama K'Opiyo was a very loving father and grandfather to his children," Mama Sarah says with a faraway look in her eyes. "Little wonder so many children were named after him."

For a long time, one of Obama K'Opiyo's wives only bore daughters. His third wife, Auma, bore many girls and only one son, Blasto Odhiambo, who was born much later. One of his daughters, Abong'o, also returned to her father's house from a failed marriage. She was *nyar lelo,* a boisterous and somewhat disruptive girl who would pick fights even with men on any contentious issue. Her father-in-law did not want her. Unperturbed, Obama took her in, nonchalantly saying that his grandchildren were many and he did not mind staying with them all in his homestead. He built a house where all the grandchildren, including the girls, would spend nights together.

But Obama K'Opiyo was not just stubborn; he was wise in the ways of his people as well. When he decided to take in his married daughter from her failed marriage, he went and called her uncles from Kanyadhiang' who cut the wood to be used for the construction of her house as required by tradition. The house was constructed at the edge of the fence near a path leading towards Ndalo's house. Her grandchildren and the girls who lived in her house would take care of her and the house as well. When she died, Abong'o was buried in her father's own homestead, again in direct contradiction of prevailing customs that decreed that a *mugogo* (married daughter) could under no circumstances be buried in her father's homestead. Very insightfully again, he made sure that her uncles from Kanyadhiang' were called to carry out the digging of the grave.

Obama K'Opiyo lived in Ka'Rachuonyo until his death. He had left Alego and never returned to that land that is now occupied by his descendants. So Opiyo and Obama K'Opiyo were buried on that other side – Ka'Rachuonyo. "Yes, where he was buried there is a stone," concluded Mama Sarah.

The descendants of Obama Opiyo have now established the Obama Opiyo Foundation. Its objective is to initiate projects to enhance the development and well being of the local community. It will also enable the international community at large to access more information about the original home of the Obama Patriarchs.

Ezra Obama and Elijah K'Obilo Obama are spearheading the activities of the Foundation. So far, the Foundation is working on two projects: a community museum to be built on the same grounds as the patriarch's mausoleum, and Obama Opiyo University. The university project is supported by Prof Shem Wandiga and Prof Peter A Odhiambo.

* * *

Just around the time that Barack Snr's father was born, the Foreign Office of the British government built the Kenya-Uganda Railway during the period when Britain maintained colonial control of the region. Construction of the line started in Mombasa in 1896 and reached Kisumu, the provincial home town of Obama Snr, in 1901. Principally, Indian labourers brought in from British India carried out the work, and many of these workers would remain in East Africa to create the substantial Indian minority communities that are still evident in Kenya and Uganda.

Some tribes, notably the Nandi led by *Orkoiyot* Koitalel arap Samoei resisted the building of the railway. The British built the railway anyway. For their troubles, the Nandi were the first tribe to be put in a native reserve.

During the early part of the century the British recruited many Africans to fight in World War I. Hussein Onyango Obama, Obama Snr's father, was among the local people who participated in this Great War.

Hussein Onyango Obama – Obama Snr's father – was born about 1895 and died in 1979. As narrated by President Barack Obama in his book, *Dreams from My Father*, as a young boy, he was restless and curious about things and would wander off for days at a time. He learnt a lot about traditional medicine and became a medicine man. In those days, traditional medicine people were highly esteemed as pharmacists, diagnosticians and doctors of the society. It was a mark of high recognition to be accepted as an acolyte by any of the established medicine people.

When the white people came, as narrated by President Barack Obama, the curiosity bug bit him hard and off he went looking for them. He eventfully reappeared wearing shirts and trousers. During that time, his people wore only animal skins and sisal fibre to cover themselves. Fearing that perhaps the coverings were meant to hide a rash, deformity or wound from circumcision, his father took no chances and warned his siblings to keep off him.

Dejected, he wandered off again and would remain estranged from his father for the rest of his life. For two weeks thereafter, he trekked all the way from his village to Nairobi, a distance of nearly 400 km, to find work. On his way he fought off a leopard with his machete and had to spend two days up a tree to keep away from a charging buffalo. In the city, he worked for some white missionaries, and when World War I broke out in 1914, he enlisted and went to fight.

He joined the war as a serviceman of the King's African Rifles (KAR) known by the locals as *askari Keya* (KAR soldiers) – a British colonial regiment formed in 1902. Its rank and file was made up of African *askaris* (servicemen), with most officers seconded from the British Army. His regiment saw action in the East African campaign against German forces. There were no roads then and all war equipment had to be carried by the KAR carrier corps, pronounced 'Kariakor' by the locals. Today, Kariakor is the name of important market locations in both Nairobi and Dar es Salaam. Hussein Onyango lived for a time in Zanzibar during his period of active service during the war. He came back a Muslim and was for a long time the only Muslim convert in his village.

In due time, Hussein Onyango Obama became a very important man to the Europeans in Ka'Rachuonyo. The Europeans would employ only Muslims as cooks, particularly because of the way they embraced hygiene. It was thus a very high honour for Hussein Onyango Obama who served as cook for a white colonial official.

As a result, Hussein Onyango Obama developed a good grasp of the white man's language and mannerisms. When the Europeans came to Ka'Rachuonyo, they always talked to him before meeting any other African. The elders greatly frowned upon this, and looked upon him as a usurper of their prerogatives. At one point, Paul Mboya, the chief elder openly rebuked him, saying: "*Okewa* (our nephew), go back to your home. What kind of man are you? Important visitors should only talk to the elders, but you are talking to the Europeans all by yourself. You cannot talk to the Europeans in Ka'Rachuonyo like this."

Still, Paul Mboya occupies pride of place in the annals of Luo history. He served as *Ker* (supreme leader) and chairman of the Luo Council of Elders. He was the first African member to sit in the Central Legislative Council (the present-day East African Parliament). He was later to gain immortality through his publication of the anthropological treatise, *Luo kitgi gi timbegi* (A handbook of Luo customs).

Hussein Onyango Obama was extremely upset with Paul Mboya, who had taken to continually ridiculing him as *ja-dak*. At one moment, a bitter Hussein Onyango told Mboya prophetically that: "You may call us mere immigrants into Ka'Rachuonyo, men without substance and with no signs of obvious success. But mark my words! One day your name will fade into oblivion, but mine, my friend, mine will be read in books and newspapers across the world!"

To save Onyango from trouble with the chief, his brothers advised him to migrate back to their ancestral land in Alego K'Ogelo in Siaya County and secure it for posterity. When he left Ka'Rachuonyo for Alego in 1939, Hussein Onyango Obama was already married to his three wives. After eighteen years of marriage to Hussein Onyango, his *Mikayi* or elder wife, Halima, had borne no children. When he made the move back to Alego, she opted to stay with her maiden family and remained in Ka'Rachuonyo. His second wife was known as Habiba Akumu *nyar* Njoga, with whom they had three children –Sarah, Barack Obama Snr, and Hawa. His third wife was Sarah Ogwel, with whom they bore seven children. Both Akumu and Mama Sarah accompanied him on the journey back to Alego.

As narrated by Peter Firstbrook in his book, *The Obamas*, John Ndalo, a close relative, says Hussein Onyango Obama actually had five wives. "There was a lady from Kawango in Mumias, for whom he even paid the bride price in several heads of cattle. Then there was Halima, followed by Sofia Odera from Karungu beyond Homa Bay in South Nyanza. Then, he married Habiba Akumu and, finally, Sarah."

When World War II broke out in 1939, Hussein Onyango Obama was called up again to join the war as a cook. This time, two of his brothers – Jotham Ndalo Obama and Blasto Odhiambo Obama – were also enlisted in the war. The family was very apprehensive about the latter's enlistment because he was the only son of his mother and it was feared that he could be a casualty of the war. The war took them to various countries in Africa, Asia and Europe. The King's African Rifles regiment in which they served fought against Mussolini's forces in Italian East Africa, against the Vichy French in Madagascar and against the Japanese during the Burma Campaign. Nevertheless, all three brothers returned home unharmed.

Hussein Onyango Obama came back from the war a changed man. He is reported to have been very fierce and fearful. He eventually separated from his second wife, Habiba Akumu *nyar* Njoga – Obama Snr's mother. After the war, he served as cook for several white families in Kenya.

In his later life, Hussein Onyango Obama only remained with his third wife, Sarah Ogwel – the now famous grandmother. Today, at an advanced age, she is still one of the busiest women around, hosting all manner of visitors who have been flocking the Obama homestead. Locally, she is affectionately known as *Dani* – Dholuo for grandmother.

Chapter 3

Birth, Childhood and Early Schooling

"We try to produce men with wisdom to seek the truth, the intelligence to find it, the humility to accept it, the courage to uphold it, and the grace to pass it on to others. By their fruits shall ye know them."
– B. L. Bowers, Principal, Maseno School (1951-1969)

Among those present at the time of Obama Snr's birth at the experienced hands of a *nyamrerwa* (traditional birth attendant) and early upbringing include his aunties – Lois Asenje, Isdorah Oyoo, Rachel Akumu, Peninah Nyangweso and Margaret Ogembo – as well as his elder cousin, Odiwa Matara. They remember him as a healthy, playful and friendly child. Until his death in April 2010, Odiwa Matara was leader of the K'Ogelo in East Africa.

Barack Hussein Obama Snr was born and grew up in a typical African village in a traditional Luo environment. He was born in 1936 in the Obama second home in K'Obama village, Rachuonyo Sub-County, Homa Bay County at the place that is now called 'Welfare K'Onyango'. The place was so-named in honour of his father, Hussein Onyango, who had donated the land for the development of a welfare centre for the local community. He was the eldest son and second born to Hussein Onyango Obama and Habiba Akumu *nyar* Njoga, the firstborn child being Sarah Nyaoke – who passed away quietly in 2007. Before her demise, Sarah Nyaoke was a politician in her own right and had worked for a local political party, Ford-Kenya, for many years.

At the time of her death, she was the secretary of the Orange Democratic Movement (ODM) party in Huruma Ward, Nairobi.

Obama Snr grew up in Ka'Rachuonyo at K'Obama Village in Southern Nyanza. He bathed in the same river where the family drew its water for domestic use – and where the animals were taken to drink. Suffice it to say that specific places were allocated for bathing, according to gender and age group, and watering the animals. As a boy, he took care of his father's goats around the family farm in K'Ogelo. He also got involved on other activities appropriate for his age and gender. Apart from working in the family farm, he would also spend some time helping with other chores in the homestead.

In a typical Luo village, the women would be up early before sunrise to fetch clean water from the river. Water for drinking had to be fetched early in the morning, after it had settled and been purified through sedimentation overnight. That done, they went out to fetch firewood. Assisted by the girls, they worked the gardens around the homestead on alternate days, especially where vegetables and lentils were grown. By midday, the women would return to the village to prepare food for the family and feed the younger children. In the evening, the young boys brought the cattle home and milked them.

At sundown, the elders would withdraw to discuss their own private matters, usually accompanied with the ritual sipping of their favourite traditional brew. On some days, especially in the harvest and post-harvest season, an expert *nyatiti* (a type of lyre) or *orutu* (a type of fiddle) singer would be in attendance, entertaining the elders with songs extolling the mores and heroes of the society. At dusk, the women would be ready with the food, and the elders sat in their respective huts to be served. Each woman in the homestead would carry her food to the elder in his hut. The sons joined their fathers to enjoy in community the food prepared in the various huts. There would be quite a variety of dishes, as some women would have cooked vegetables, others fish, meat or chicken, in all assuring one of a hearty meal and a balanced diet.

The repast over, the children sat at the feet of the elders, or gathered in the hut of the chief village elder and listened to whatever they had to say. It was an opportunity for the young to learn and be prepared for their future. This was a traditional system of education. The elders would instruct the boys about everyday duties and instill in them manly virtues, or they would instruct them through stories, myths and legends. At the same time, the young girls would sit at the feet of their mothers and grandmothers, telling stories and learning about women's roles in the society. They would compete in finding solutions to riddles and tongue twisters, and the elder women would regale them with tantalising stories about the history and adventures of their ancestors.

* * *

Barack Obama Snr started school at Seventh Day Adventist Church-sponsored Gendia Primary School in Kendu Bay, South Nyanza. This was before the family migrated to Alego in Central Nyanza. After the family moved back to Alego, he continued schooling at Nyang'oma in K'Ogelo Village, then proceeded to Ng'iya Intermediate School in Siaya County. Mama Sarah gives a brief history of the school in K'Ogelo.

"The school, started by the Roman Catholic Church, operated under a tree and comprised of a few choice rocks for sitting on," Mama Sarah explains. "It was next to a road, making learning an exercise in concentration. Whenever a car passed by, the children would get distracted, since cars were quite a novelty in the village then. Some of them would go running after the cars, shouting excitedly and claiming the cars for their own. The hapless teacher would be left standing alone, not knowing what to do."

The school that he attended is now called Senator Obama Secondary School. "It was renamed after Barack Obama was elected to the Senate," Mama Sarah says. "It is now an established school with both primary and secondary sections. But it all started under a tree."

There were many incidences at school. In Nyang'oma, he never went up to Primary Two. In those days, 'discipline' consisted of a few choice strokes of the cane administered straight to the buttocks, which would preferably be bared for maximum impact. He put his foot down: there was no way a female teacher could 'discipline' him! In fact, he adamantly refused to attend any school where there were women teachers. He was a man, and there was no way that a woman could teach him – the way they teach nursery school children!

He rather preferred to walk – barefoot – to Ng'iya, some 7 km away, where he could be taught by men and punished by men, if necessary. He would walk the distance and never got late for school. In the rainy season when walking was particularly difficult on account of the muddy conditions, he would come back from school dog-tired, eat his supper quietly and go straight to sleep.

Samson Chilo Were was Obama Snr's teacher at Ng'iya Primary School and is now advanced in age. He recalls that the classrooms were just mud huts and the children walked barefoot; nevertheless Obama Snr was a smart boy; very clever in class.[10] Magdalene Otin, one of the few ladies to have been taken to school by her parents those days, shared a class with Obama Snr at Ng'iya. She remembers that Obama Snr liked football.

Caleb Omogi, later to become one of Kenya's long-serving diplomats, was one of Obama Snr's earliest friends. He knew Obama Snr well from his younger days – in 1948. That was before he went to Maseno. "He was a brilliant and very naughty boy," he comments with a chuckle.

Peter Oloo Aringo, a long time cabinet minister in the Kenya government, was another youthful friend of Obama Snr They hailed from the same neighbourhood. "I have known Oloo Aringo for a long time," says Mama Sarah. "... sometimes they would come as late as 2 a.m. and I had to give them something to eat before they went to sleep."

After he successfully completed his primary school at Ng'iya, Obama Snr proceeded to Maseno School for his secondary education. There, he continued his good run, doing well in his studies as he had done before.

Whereas his academic performance was commendable, there are strong indications that he ran into some trouble regarding his social life and on matters of discipline. Such would eventually lead to his expulsion before he could finish his studies at Maseno.

---

[1] Peter Firstbrook, *The Obamas*, p. 180.

Dr Francis Masakhalia gives a brief background about Barack's life at the Maseno School where he and Barack were classmates. "As an Anglican missionary school, a cardinal principle of the institution was to turn over to the nation educated young people with impeccable credentials of honesty, good character and integrity. The school had two services every day – in the morning before breakfast and in the evening before dinner." During these services, matters of faith and character were preached. The headmaster, Mr Mayor, a Cambridge University graduate, used the school assembly and services to name those who excelled, the good, and the naughty.

John Oywa, who interviewed the Maseno School's senior teacher in charge of archives, Mangla Okanda, confirms that the school maintains records for all students who have passed through its gates since its founding in 1906. These include prominent Kenyans such as Kenya's first vice-president, Jaramogi Oginga Odinga and freedom fighter Ramogi Achieng' Oneko. Obama Snr's records at the school are also intact. "He joined the school in 1950 and left in 1953," Okanda explains. He was admitted by B L Bowers, who served as principal of the school from 1951 to 1969. He was registered with index no. 3422. He joined the school together with his elder brother or cousin, Joseph, who left in 1951 for unclear reasons.

School records depict him as an excellent student and show that he was promoted from Class B to A. "This is an indication that he was a brilliant boy, since Class A was reserved for the very bright students," says Okanda. The principal describes him as "very keen, steady, trustworthy and friendly ... concentrates, reliable and outgoing". The classroom where he studied is still intact.[11]

Even though he maintained top grades throughout his studies, Obama Snr never finished school at Maseno.

As his schoolmate at Maseno and one-time Kenya's Minister for Finance, Dr Masakhalia says, he was expelled on the grounds of indiscipline.

---

[2] John Oywa, *East African Standard*, 11 April 2008. Available from: http://www.standardmedia. co.ke/obama/InsidePage.php?id=1143998493&cid=530&. (Accessed 20 December 2014].

* * *

Maseno town lies squarely on the equator, atop a hill in Nyanza, some 17 miles (about 27 km) from Kisumu City. It affords a spectacular view of Lake Victoria, which is just 12 miles (about 19 km) away in an area of rich and beautiful slopping countryside. To this date, there is in Maseno an old, withered fig tree, an odd site indeed. It had been split down the middle by lightning. A prop supports one of its grotesque limbs and its heart is black and charred. Next to the tree is a lovely church built of stone with a cool thatched roof designed to withstand the vagaries of the tropical climate.

Only a few yards separate the tree and the church but, between them, they represent centuries of paganism and its succession by a century of Christianity and educational advancement. For they are the twin focal points of the Mission School at Maseno, which has grown from nothing to one of the largest and most advanced educational establishments in Kenya. By the fig tree, the CMS missionary, later Bishop J J Willis, built a grass hut, showing complete disregard for the ancient local superstition that the tree was the abode of evil spirits and scene of grotesque ancient sacrificial ceremonies. It is from this old fig tree that Maseno gets its name.

In retrospect, the rich history of Maseno School dates back to the October/November period of 1900, when a young missionary on his way to Uganda passed through Nyanza on a bicycle followed by a cheering crowd of naked Africans. A man sitting on wheels and going faster than a man could run? Never before had they seen anything so strange! Struck by the friendliness of the people, the young missionary, J J Willis of the Church Missionary Society (CMS), strongly felt himself called to win them to Christ. Five years later, he returned – to start a missionary outpost in the area. He chose Maseno for his base.[12] After he had acquired the basics of *Dholuo* (Luo language), Bishop J J Willis started the school in 1906 in a small mud and wattle hut with four boys for learners.

By 1907, the school had 12 pupils. The growth was slow at the beginning because the idea of paying for education seemed outrageous to the local people.

---

[3] Kenya National Archives, documents on the early history of Maseno School.

Despite the slow start, Maseno was destined to become a base from which the Christian gospel would be preached far and wide into the surrounding country. Today, the impact of Maseno is felt far and wide – as far as the USA – in the hallowed precincts of the White House itself.

Times were difficult and diseases rampant. Supplies for building and food for the schools had to be transported from Kisumu, some 17 miles (about 27 km) away, on the heads and shoulders of porters. In 1908, the foundations for Maseno church were laid at the centre of the compound and, ever since, it has served as the school chapel and pastorate church. Teachers, lay readers and evangelists trained here preached the gospel far and wide. By 1920, it had a primary school and teacher training section where more than 120 boys were instructed in building, carpentry, printing, tailoring, telegraphy, medicine and clerical work.

Sunday services those days attracted young warriors in war paint and colourful feathers, riding on bullocks. They came to dance to God. The idea of kneeling in prayer was utterly foreign to them. How could the spirits hear them if they did not make plenty of noise? Bishop J J Willis had his own worries. There is a tale that when he left Uganda, he was presented with a bale of cheap cloth to clothe the people he was going to evangelise. Upon his arrival in Maseno, he was embarrassed to see all the people walking around his house, stark naked. He gave each African a ration of cloth but, to his surprise, they made it into hats!

In his memoirs, *My Footprints in the Sands of Time*, reknowned historian Prof Bethwell Ogot provides further background on the development of Maseno School. When Edward Carey Francis arrived at Maseno on 26 October 1928 to become the principal of the school, he found the literary side of education badly neglected. Unimpressed, he decided to put more emphasis on literary education. Due to his diligence, the Church Missionary Society (CMS) Maseno School was authorised to start a junior secondary course in 1938, thus becoming the third African secondary school in the country after Alliance High School and Mangu. The area around Maseno has over the years grown into a major educational hub. Today, apart from the school, Maseno University with a population of thousands of students is another unique educational institution that has developed in the locality.

From the beginning, Maseno School had a strong moral foundation and objective. As one former headmaster of the school, B L Bowers put it: "We try to produce men with wisdom to seek the truth, the intelligence to find it, the humility to accept it, the courage to uphold it, and the grace to pass it on to others. By their fruits shall ye know them." Today, you know one of them: Barack Hussein Obama, the 44th President of the United States of America is – through his father – one of the fruits of this great institution.

Chapter 4

Son of Two Mothers

"An wuod Akumu nyar Njoga kod Sarah Ogwel"
(I am the son of Akumu nyar Njoga and Sarah Ogwel)
– Barack Obama Snr

Though the thunder has been stolen by Sarah Obama, Obama Snr's living stepmother, the biological African grandmother's picture of Habiba Akumu *nyar* Njoga, holding her son Obama Snr adorns the cover of her grandson's, President Barack Obama's best-selling book, *Dreams from My Father*.

As it were, Habiba had separated from her husband, Hussein Onyango Obama, when Obama Snr was just nine years old. At the time of her divorce, she had three children, two others having died earlier. In her subsequent marriage, she got several other children. We traced her relatives and interviewed them at length. This is her story.

The story of Obama Snr's biological mother, Habiba Akumu *nyar* Njoga was narrated by several close relatives. These included Cleopa Nyang'aye, her cousin who is now advanced in age, and her younger sister, Stella Juma Nyaboi from Karabondi. Also recounting her story was Mwana Hawa Auma Magak, her daughter from the first marriage and the sole surviving sister of Obama Snr. Other sources included Habiba's three children from her second marriage – her two sons Amir Otieno Orinda and Razik Salmin Madoro and their sister, Zarifa Akello Miragi who passed on during the course of writing this book.

According to her cousin, *Mzee* Cleopa Nyang'aye, Habiba Akumu *nyar* Njoga was born to John Njoga and his wife Bwogi *nyar* Otore –

also known as *nyar* Nyakach, from where she hailed. *Nyar* Njoga, as she was popularly known, hailed from the Wandhidhi clan who live around Simbi Nyaima in Karabondi Location. Their original home was in Kanyaluo, Kosele, also in Rachuonyo Sub-County. She was the firstborn in a Christian family of the Seventh Day Adventist faith. She did not have any formal education.

In a sworn affidavit before the Resident Magistrate in Siaya on Monday 20 August 1984 during the battle for Barack Obama Snr's estate, Habiba Akumu *nyar* Njoga states in part:

> *My name is Asha Akumu Orinda. I was born at Karabondi sub-location, Kokela Village, East Ka'Rachuonyo Location, in South Nyanza. My father's name is Njoga son of Okela of Karabondi, Karachuonyo. I currently live in K'Owuor sub-location, Ong'ang Village, South Karachuonyo (Kanyaluo) in South Nyanza. I was first married in East Alego, K'Ogelo, Nyang'oma where I stayed for several years and then broke the marriage and later got married at Wagwe, Karachuonyo, South Nyanza. Hussein Onyango Obama was my first husband and Salmin Orinda was the second husband. My children by Hussein Onyango Obama are Sarah Nyaoke, Dr Hussein Barack Obama, Mwana Hawa Auma, Rashid Ndalo, and Adhil Fwata. Only two of my children from that union, Sarah Nyaoke and Mwana Hawa Auma are still alive ...*

In her prime, Akumu was a ravishing beauty. She met her husband, Hussein Onyango Obama, in the 1930s. A veteran of World War I, Hussein Onyango had a fearsome reputation. He lost no time in sweeping the beautiful girl off her feet – quite literally.

"My father met my mother in the local market and fell for her irresistible beauty. She was very light-skinned," says Mwana Hawa, the sole surviving daughter from that union. "There was no matchmaking. He married her by force!" That was the Luo customary *meko* or 'marriage by capture'.

After their marriage, she was given a Muslim name, Habiba. She bore him several children – the first born, Sarah, followed by Barack

Obama Snr and the third born, Hawa. She and her children lived with Halima, the first wife, in Obama K'Opiyo's homestead in Ka'Nyadhiang Location in Kendu Bay.

Later on, *Mzee* Nyang'aye adds, they travelled to Uganda where Hussein Onyango had gone to work. In Uganda, they were blessed with some more children, but they died under unexplained circumstances, most likely from an epidemic that swept through the land. The couple later returned to Kenya.

Sometimes after they had returned from Uganda, she was involved in a serious row with her husband. This elicited a bad reaction from her family and her father who was a friend to the then area chief, Paul Mboya. Hussein was already under pressure to move from the Sub-County. It was thus agreed that Hussein Onyango should move away from their midst. He obliged and migrated together with his family to Alego K'Ogelo in Siaya County, where they settled. Soon thereafter, he left for World War II.

According to Mwana Hawa, her parents' marriage broke down due to her father's hostile socialisation during the war.

"After his service in the army, our father came back a changed man. He was very hostile and the village people feared him," she says. "He was very harsh and nobody dared cross his path. When we were children, he would beat us senseless. Mother would not intervene – she would receive a thorough beating herself if she dared."

Habiba had a very troubled marriage with her husband. She found Onyango too demanding. He would always find fault with her and her ways. He was even stricter with her regarding the children who, he insisted, had to be brought up under the strictest regimen of discipline.

He brought fancy clothes from the city which the children were expected to put on all the time and that had to remain spotlessly clean. She turned to her co-wife, Halima, who tried to help her with the children. Still, she continued to struggle and generally remained unhappy and discontented.

She tried to leave her husband more than once – first after Sarah was born, and again after Obama Snr's birth. Despite his pride, Onyango followed her. Both times, Habiba's family took his side, so she had no choice but to return. In the meantime, she quietly clung to her bitterness and bided her time.

Habiba never gave up her persistent attempts to escape. A serious and violent quarrel with her husband was the last straw.

One night, when her daughter Sarah Nyaoke was 12 years and Obama Snr nine years, she finally made her move. She had long endured a difficult marriage to her husband; now was her chance to bolt for it. She had decided to run away and go back to her parents in Kendu, hundreds of miles away. Waking up in the dead of the night, she hoarsely whispered her tearful byes to the children. She hurriedly informed them about her decision, but warned that it was still dark and the journey perilous. For their own safety, the children could only join her later, some day. Then she disappeared into the thick darkness.

When Hussein Onyango Obama woke up, the hut was unusually quiet. The children were gloomy, and attempts to question them only brought forth tears and sobs. When he finally figured out the situation, he was furious. Perhaps, he thought, he should finally let Akumu go – so persistent had been her attempts to escape from the marriage. But when he saw how young the children really were, and that even Mama Sarah, with two children of her own, was little more than a girl, he again resolved to go after his wife.

Dutifully, he went to Akumu's family in Kendu and asked that she be returned. This time around, his luck ran out. The family flatly refused to entertain his pleas. In fact, they had already accepted dowry for her remarriage to another man, and Akumu and her new husband had left for Tanganyika (now mainland Tanzania). There was nothing Hussein Onyango could do, so he returned to Alego empty-handed. Arriving home, he issued his new policy: henceforth, Mama Sarah would be the mother of all his children. And that was that.

Habiba was remarried to Salmin Orinda, a Muslim from Wagwe near Homa Hills, South Nyanza. She was renamed Asha to avoid confusion since her new mother-in-law also bore the name Habiba. Later, they migrated to Kosele, Ka'Rachuonyo, where her new husband had acquired a parcel of land. They were eventually blessed with more children. Despite the gravity of the situation and the rift it created, she maintained contact with her children by Hussein Onyango, but she never returned to her erstwhile matrimonial home.

According to her son Amir – now a retired teacher from the local Kendu Muslim Primary School in Rachuonyo Sub-County – Habiba Akumu *nyar* Njoga's contribution has not been properly acknowledged. She was a hard-working woman who also spared a thought for posterity. One of her last wishes was for the family to start a community project in her memory. They planted a forest. "She wanted us to start a memorial place whereby anybody visiting her grave could see the work of her hands," says Amir. "We started the forest project in accordance with her wishes."

In her heyday, Habiba Akumu *nyar* Njoga was active in grass roots-level politics. Even though she did not venture into mainstream politics, she was forthright in fighting for the rights of the disadvantaged. She was also a strong community mobiliser. She had political and leadership talent as well, adds Amir. She was leader of the *Peke* Kendu Muslim Women Group. She led the group from rural obscurity to celebrity status; it soon became the most sought after entertainment troupe in the region. Her leadership was instrumental in that makeover. She straddled the whole expanse of the political divide as she kept politics out of business. She related well with both Phoebe Asiyo and Lazarus Amayo, the two political titans who were then involved in political combat for the Ka'Rachuonyo Constituency seat in Nyanza. Her troupe was engaged by both political camps on the campaign trail.

Due to rampant poverty that stalked the land, she came up with innovative ways of empowering women, especially on food production and income-generating activities. She often visited agricultural extension officers to learn new ways of farming, and would gladly pass on the information so gained to fellow women. She also had considerable knowledge of herbal remedies, which enabled her to treat many people of various ailments. She was an accomplished traditional birth attendant. Besides the normal activities at the local level, Akumu *nyar* Njoga had a keen interest in education. She would encourage her neighbours and friends to send their children to school as a way of investing in their future and often gave her son as a good example of the fruits of education.

One of her most significant traits was a very high sense of civic awareness. She constantly reminded her fellow women to safeguard their voter's cards in the same manner that they safeguarded their national identity cards. This, she emphasised, was the only way they could guarantee their future through a conscientious exercise of their democratic prerogative. She voted religiously in every election herself.

* * *

Sarah Obama is currently the best known 'Obama' due to her direct link with President Barack Obama. Sarah, due to fate and her magnanimity has become the darling of many and her home has become a tourist attraction. Sarah brought up Obama Senior and his siblings after his mother divorced his father. Though this is the norm in an African polygamous setting, nonetheless she did an excellent job of raising her own six children and her co-wife's three others. The enormity of raising nine children with meagre resources cannot be overemphasised. She strived to educate all the children. It was her tenacity and love for the children that translated into fruition and academic excellence as exemplified by her stepson, the late Barack Obama Snr.

Sarah Omar Ogwel of Wagwe is the third wife of Hussein Onyango Obama. She is the biological mother of six children – Onyango, Zeituni, Yusuf, Said, Marsat and Ojijo. Whereas she brought him up, Sarah was not Obama Snr's biological mother. As the youngest wife, she spent the most time with Onyango Obama, staying with him in his town house in Nairobi, while her two co-wives, Halima and Habiba, lived in their grandfather's homestead in Kendu. When Habiba divorced Obama, the responsibility of taking care of her three children fell on her. By that time, Mama Sarah had relocated upcountry as well, and stayed in Hussein Onyango Obama's homestead in Nyang'oma K'Ogelo in Siaya.

But the children of Habiba Akumu while still staying with Sarah missed their mother and made an attempt to follow her. Obama Snr was only nine years old when his mother, Habiba Akumu *nyar* Njoga, divorced his father, abandoning him as well. Luckily for him, his step-mother, Sarah Ogwel, took him in and raised him.

At one point in their escape attempt, they managed to leave the homestead, but they did not go far before their plans unravelled. After walking for some distance, they lost their way and ended up in a stranger's home along the way. The lady of the home where they eventually ended up welcomed them, and then she carefully questioned them about their family name and their mission. Before she sent them back home, they innocently told her that they had run away from Alego, and were headed for their maternal grandfather's home near Simbi Nyaima in Ka'Rachuonyo. Back in Alego, the children later made a second attempt to escape. They remembered their mother's instructions, and only a few weeks passed before Sarah woke up her brother in the middle of the night, just as her mother had done to her. She hushed him, helped him get dressed, and together they began the long walk on the road to Kendu. It is a wonder that they both survived.

They were gone for almost two weeks, walking miles every day, hiding from those who passed them on the road, sleeping rough in the fields and scrounging for food. At one moment, they were nearly attacked by a ferocious hippo tending to her young. Not far from Kendu, they lost their way. An old woman found them huddled together, crying. She took pity on them, for they were filthy and starved. She took them in, fed them and asked them their names. Once she understood their kin and lineage, she took them to their village in Kendu. When Hussein Onyango Obama eventually came and set his eyes on them and took in their sorry state, he cried long and bitterly. The children never tried to run away again.

In a way Obama Snr was wild and stubborn – just like his mother. On the other hand, the personality of his sister Sarah was in many ways like that of her father: strict, hard-working and quick to anger. By saving part of her income, Mama Sarah helped pay for Obama Snr's education as he grew up. Any time she required money for his school fees, she would take one of her cows to the market and sell it off. She only spent part of the proceeds on family upkeep, saving the rest to pay for his education. She would also harvest beans and raise money by selling them in the market.

"Those days I used to ride my bicycle," she chuckles. "When the harvest was plentiful, I would look for somebody to help me take the beans to the market. We would tie our produce on our bicycle and ride to Ndere market, where a sack of beans would go for Kshs 60 (just about 60 US cents), while the small ones would cost Kshs 20." Her husband, Hussein Onyango Obama, was away most of the time working in the city as a domestic servant for British settlers. Whenever he came home for the holidays, he would be surprised at the amazing progress made in schooling the children.

Mama Sarah well remembers the time when Obama Snr went missing as a child. At that time, his father had come from Nairobi and was keen to inspect his sons' progress in school by checking his books. That morning, he left home with a friend to go to school, but never returned in the evening. The next day, the family was beside itself, looking for him all over. Seeing no trace of him, his distraught father reported the matter to the school. Upon further inquiries, some information came to light. The lad had been seen leaving the vicinity with a certain woman in tow. That night, his father never slept a wink. Before sunrise the next morning, he saddled his bicycle and left for Ng'iya, the local market. He quickly traced the boys who would lead him to his son's hideout. True enough, he found him – doing manual work in someone's farm. His son had been hired as a labourer!

The old man's tears flowed freely; so piteous was the sight. He could scarcely believe that the emaciated, scraggly and ill-clad lad before him was his beloved son. Sensing danger, the woman who had hired him launched into a tirade of excuses, and then quietly slunk away. Too angry to speak, Hussein Onyango Obama quietly helped the errant young man onto the bicycle and brought him home. He proceeded to cut his unkempt hair and had him scrubbed good. He did not beat or punish him in any way.

Later Ogembo, his friend, would say: "Whenever he was with his friends in social places, Obama Snr was fond of invoking the names of his two mothers, reminding them that he was the proud son of two mothers – Habiba Akumu *nyar* Njoga and Sarah Ogwel". That was his characteristic vaunt in social places.

Chapter 5

Early Working Life and First Marriage

---

*"The first time you marry for love, the second for money, and
the third for companionship."*
- Jackie Kennedy

Obama Snr married four times and had a total of eight children. His
wives in respective order are Grace Kezia Aoko (Kenyan), Stanley
Ann Dunham (American), Ruth Beatrice Baker (American), and Jael
Atieno (Kenyan). His children are Roy Malik Abong'o, Rita Auma,
Samson Nyandega, Bernard Otieno (all by Kezia); President Barack
Hussein Obama (by Ann); Mark Okoth and David Opiyo (by Ruth) and
George Hussein Onyango (by Jael).

Obama Snr's first wife, Kezia, is a Kenyan and has in-laws of Russian
origin. His daughter, Auma, got married to a Briton while his son, Malik
first married an American. Obama Snr's second marriage was to an
American, Ann Dunham – whose parents are of Irish and German descent.
She later divorced him and remarried Lolo Soetoro, an Indonesian with
whom they bore a daughter, Maya Kassandra Soetoro, who is now
married to a Chinese-Canadian. Obama Snr's wife by the third marriage,
Ruth, is an American of Jewish extraction. She later divorced him and
got remarried – to a Kenyan of Tanzanian origin, Simeon Ndesandjo.
Ruth's son, Mark Ndesandjo, is married to a Chinese and lives in the
Peoples' Republic of China, where he was named the image ambassador
in 2009. After his death, Obama Snr's fourth wife Jael Atieno lived for
a while with a Frenchman, Christian Bertrand, in Nairobi, with whom
they had plans to get married. She later moved to South Korea where

she met and got married to Hosea Dixon, an African-American who was then serving in the US military base in South Korea.[1] With this kind of a global family, it is no wonder President Barack Obama said: "I have brothers, sisters, nieces, nephews, uncles and cousins, of every race and every hue, scattered across three continents ... when we get together for Christmas or thanksgiving, it's like a mini United Nations."

In his book, *Dreams from My Father*, President Barack Obama talks passionately about his brother, Abong'o Malik Obama, then known as Roy. Recalling the events of his wedding where his brother was the best man, the President says, "The person who made me proudest of all, though, was Roy ... he looked so dignified in his black African gown with white trim and matching cap that some of our guests mistook him for my father."[2] Kezia's first born son, Abong'o Malik Obama, released a biography about his father entitled, *Barack Obama Snr: The Rise and Life of a True African Scholar*, published by Xlibris (2012).

Kezia's second born child and only daughter, Dr Auma Obama, has written her autobiography published in German and later translated into English by Ross Benjamin under the title, *And Then Life Happens: A Memoir*. The book follows the life of the two siblings who grew up in two ends of the world but have a common father, how they meet, the exploration of family history and finally the support of his brother on his way to the US presidency. The initial book was launched in Munich on 14 October 2010, where Afro-fusion star Suzzanna Owiyo from Kenya gave a sizzling performance.

* * *

When Obama Snr was expelled from school at Maseno, his father arranged for him a job in Mombasa. He had little choice, for the old man brooked no dissent. He took up the job in the office of an Arab merchant. After a short time, however, he had an argument with his boss and left in a huff. He found another job as a clerk, but it paid much less. He was too proud to ask his father for help or admit he had been wrong.

---

[1] George Obama (with Damien Lewis), *Homeland*, pp. 20, 236.
[2] Barack Obama, *Dreams from My Father*, p. 441.

Nevertheless, word got back to Hussein Onyango Obama, and when he came home for a visit, his father berated him, in his anger shouting that he would amount to nothing. He remonstrated with his father, arguing that the new job paid much better than the first one. He said that he was earning one hundred and fifty shillings every month. The old man was wiser by a mile. "Let me see your wage book, if you are such a wealthy man," he demanded. Outflanked, he lowered his gaze and kept mum. His father knew right away that he had lied. He retreated to his hut and told the errant son to go away because he had brought shame on his father.

In the mid-1950s, Obama Snr found a job working as a clerk for the railway corporation. After he got married, he came to Nairobi accompanied by his wife Kezia. At 18 and living in Alego, Siaya County, Obama Snr returned to visit his relatives in Ka'Rachuonyo, in Rachuonyo District, where he met a 16-year old schoolgirl, Kezia Atieno. She was at home for her school holidays.

"It was at a dance in Kendu Bay, my home town," Kezia remembers. "I went to the dance hall with my cousin William and I saw him enter the room. I thought, 'Oh, wow!' He was so lovely with his dancing ... so handsome and smart. We danced together and then the next day my cousin came to our house and told me that Barack liked me ..."

"It was December, so I was off school," adds Kezia. "About a week later, William and I took Barack to the station. When the train arrived William and Barack said, 'You are going to Nairobi.' I went with him." Her father and brothers came to Nairobi to bring her so she could continue with school, but she would hear none of it.[3] Despite some initial resistance from close family members, including Hussein Onyango Obama, the two were married one year later – in January 1957.

Accompanied by his cousin Tom Deya, Elijah K'Obilo formed part of the delegation that delivered the dowry. They drove the cows to Kezia's maiden home, just across the River Awach in Rachuonyo District.

---

[3] Elizabeth Sanderson, *Daily Mail,* 6 January 2008. Available at: http://www.dailymail.co.uk/news/article-506338/Barack-Obamas-stepmother-living-Bracknell-reveals-close-bond---mother.html#ixzz0atsxVBAP (Accessed: 20 December 2013].

The newly married couple set up home in Nairobi. They had two children in quick succession. The first son, Roy Abong'o, was born in March 1958. The second born, Rita Auma, would follow within two years.

Apparently his love for dancing that led to his meeting Kezia did not stop with their first dance. Mama Sarah confirmed that, as a young man, Obama Snr won many dancing competitions. His love of music was part of the rich lore of the Luo. Even after marriage, he did not stop dancing. "We used to carry our first born baby, Malik, with us and we would put him to sleep in a cot as we danced," Kezia reported. He also took her out for live band performances as far away as Kendu Bay.[4]

They stayed with one of his cousins in Makongeni, Nairobi, where they occupied Block F20 no 6. Having acquired independent means of his own, the family moved to block F20 no 10 where they lived with their two children, Malik and Auma. They later moved to Ofafa Maringo. According to her sister-in-law Rhoda Anyango, he led a lavish lifestyle and enjoyed the company of progressive thinkers who encouraged him to excel.

* * *

The Nairobi of the 1950s was a city under siege. The British colonial administration maintained a vice-like grip on the emerging city, and all social and economic organisation mirrored the unequal power relations. The city centre was reserved for government buildings and was out of bounds for Africans, unless they could prove that they had legitimate business there. Living quarters too were racially segregated. The northern parts of the city was reserved for whites, the Asians mainly occupied the western part, while the poorer Eastlands section was the preserve of Africans.

The Eastlands estate of Makongeni was owned by the railways corporation, while Kaloleni, Mbotela and Shauri Moyo were run by the Nairobi City Council. It was around this time that Obama Snr met two American ladies, Elizabeth Mooney Kirk and Helen M. Roberts, who encouraged him to go for further studies abroad. Elizabeth Kirk was an international literacy expert then working in Kenya.

---

4 John Oywa, "Kezia Obama: My Life with Obama Senior" *East African Standard*, 11 September 2008.

She had been hired to help the Kenya Department of Education set up a literacy programme funded by the USA International Cooperation Administration (ICA), an arm of the USA Department of State that administered development aid. Her brief included the development of a countrywide literacy campaign that used the local languages as a stepping stone to achieving English language proficiency.

In due course, she brought together a sort of project support team who helped run the programme. They also helped her to develop elementary reading materials in the local languages.

Obama Snr worked for her as part of that team, starting off as an office assistant who also handled basic writing and translation duties. And so it was in that context that he wrote his first book, *Otieno Jarieko* (Otieno the Wise Man). A few others would soon follow. Perhaps in appreciation of his nascent potential, Elizabeth encouraged Obama Snr to pursue education by correspondence, an advice that he took to heart, and that eventually bore fruit when later he was accepted for further education in Hawaii.

He started learning by correspondence in an effort to secure a Cambridge School Certificate, which would enable him qualify for further studies abroad. But he was soon involved in the politics of the country, which took a lot of his time.

The Mau Mau war was on in full swing and the land was restive. Everywhere, there were charged rallies calling for the release of Jomo Kenyatta, the detained nationalist leader. He began to attend political meetings after work and in that way got introduced to some leaders of the nationalist party, Kenya African National Union (KANU). It was such activities that earned him a brief stint in detention at one time. He continued working hard on his studies by correspondence until he passed his examinations.

Obama Senior stayed with his new wife until 1959, when he left for Hawaii, leaving his wife Kezia three months pregnant with Auma. Besides his son Roy, he was to have two other sons by her – Abo in 1968 and Bernard in 1970.

In later years, Kezia relocated to Bracknell, England. Present to celebrate his 2005 inauguration as Senator for Illinois, she is a living witness to the great significance of the stupendous achievement of Barack Obama's son. She also joined the tearful throng of people who witnessed the epoch-making inauguration of Barack Obama Snr's scion as the 44th President of the USA on 20 January 2008.

Chapter 6

Quest for Further Education and Second Marriage

"How can you marry this white woman when you have responsibilities at home? Will this woman return with you and live as a Luo woman? Will she accept that you already have a wife and children? I have not heard of white people understanding such things. Their women are jealous and are used to being pampered."

– Hussein Onyango Obama

Being a stellar student, it was not long before Obama Snr was offered a scholarship to the USA. In the summer of 1959, he joined the University of Hawaii Economics Department where he aced his exams, maintaining an A-grade throughout.

His airfare was paid with the support of the Elizabeth Kirk and Helen M. Roberts, who provided a partial scholarship. Tom Mboya of the famous airlift put him on the African-American Student Foundation (AASF) list for possible funding, which he later got.[1] By the summer of 1959, he was bound for Hawaii. In what came to be known in Kenya as the 'Tom Mboya airlifts', an estimated 800 students went to America for studies between 1958 and 1962.[2]

Mboya himself had made his first trip to America in 1957 in what was the first step towards the organisation of the airlifts.

The project was conceived out of the realisation that the impending Kenyan independence needed a large stock of well-educated Kenyans to serve in the public as well as private sectors. "Nothing constitutes a

---

[1] Tom Shachtman, *Airlift to America*, p. x. See also David Goldsworthy, *Tom Mboya: The Man Kenya Wanted to Forget*, p. 61 (East African Educational Publishers).

[2] Tom Shachtman, *Airlift to America*, p. x (St Martin's Press, New York, 2009).

greater contribution to the struggle against poverty, disease and political subjection in Africa more than the contribution made towards our peoples' educational advancement," Mboya penned in a letter to *The New York Times* on 8 November 1959.

The original idea of the airlifts was conceived several years prior to Kenya's independence. It was initially the brainchild of two prominent Kenyans; Tom Mboya and Julius Gikonyo Kiano, both of whom later served as cabinet ministers in post-independence Kenya.

At the time, Mboya was a trade unionist leading the Kenya Federation of Labour, an outfit he had helped establish. Kiano, on the other hand, had just returned from the USA, where he had graduated with a PhD. Together with the American industrialist-cum-philanthropist, William Scheinman, they mobilised prominent personalities and organisations in the United States to fund the project.

For his maiden tour, Tom Mboya was sponsored by the American Committee on Africa (ACOA), an organisation of Americans interested in furthering American-African relations in Africa that had been formed in 1953. The ACOA executive and advisory boards included several well-known black leaders of the time – such as Adam Clayton Powell, A Phillip Randolph and Bayard Rustin.

Mboya arrived in New York on 15 August 1957 – his 26th birthday. He held a series of meetings with prominent personalities in the USA from which he came up with important deals within a very short time. He successfully negotiated for a training programme in America for African unionists and the building of labour centres in Kenya by the Americans. So began a new phase in his career that was to accrue crucial political importance and earn him powerful enemies at home.

Perhaps most important of all, Mboya made contact with William X Scheinman, head of Anrav Industries, a firm which manufactured aircraft components – who introduced him to Senator John F Kennedy (later US President) and other American political figures. He served on the executive board of the American Committee on Africa, and in 1959, together with Mboya established the AASF, which raised funds to take hundreds of Kenyans to study at American universities from 1957 to 1961. They struck up a friendship, and discussed at length the possibility of Americans paying airfares for African students from Kenya so that they could take up places offered by American colleges. In the next few months, Scheinman personally paid for 17 Kenyan students. Thus was the idea of the student airlifts born and nurtured.

According to Dr Francis Masakhalia, a former Minister for Finance in the Kenya government and former schoolmate of Obama Snr at Maseno, Mboya and his associates started organising for the first student airlift in 1958. In the following year, he launched a movement for education overseas and helped found the AASF. Obama Snr became one of the beneficiaries.

Frank Montero, the then president of the AASF as well as Scheinman, the then vice-president, and Jackie Robinson – all played important roles in securing funding for the airlift between 1959 and 1960. Mboya also made contact with civil rights leader, Martin Luther King Jr., African-American trade unionist Phillip Randolph and USA actor Sidney Poitier.

In his autobiography, *Freedom and After*, Tom Mboya acknowledged Gordon Hagberg of the Institute of International Education (IIE) for his description of the airlift as well as *Harper*'s Magazine and the Atlantic for their comments on the airlift. His wife, Gloria Hagberg, who died in Kenya in June 2010, also played a major part in the airlifts. With her husband, Gordon Hagberg, they helped the Kenyan students go to America during the airlifts between 1958 and 1962. She conducted pre-airlift classes for students who had qualified for the scholarships on the realities of life as students in a foreign country.

Writing in *The Washington Post*, Michael Dobbs reports that a letter among the Mboya Papers at Stanford University's Hoover Institution shows most of Obama Snr's early expenses in the United States were covered by Elizabeth Mooney Kirk, an international literacy expert who travelled widely in Kenya. Kirk wrote to Mboya in 1962 requesting for funds to sponsor Obama Snr for graduate studies at Harvard. Funds provided the following year by John F Kennedy's family paid off old debts and subsidised student stipends, therefore indirectly benefiting Obama Snr. Odinge Odera who was part of the airlift has given details of the flight in his book, *My Journey with Jaramogi*. He says, "Our journey started on the evening of 6 September 1959, on a TurboProp Aircraft which made stops in Khartoum in Sudan, Benghazi, Libya; Rome, Italy; London, England; Shanon, Ireland; Ganda, Nova Scotia, Canada, and finally New York City's Idlewild Airport (now JFK Airport). As Remnick puts it, most of the eighty-one members of the 1959 airlift class from Kenya came together on a single charter flight from Nairobi to New York with refuelling stops along the way. Obama Snr took a different flight. "But he certainly is considered part of the contingent," says Cora Weiss, executive director of the programme. "We wrote cheques for his tuition, books and clothes."[3]

The beneficiaries of the airlifts included stellar personalities of independent Kenya. Among the top executives who benefited included Joe Wanjui (industrialist and vice chancellor, University of Nairobi); Prof Wangari Maathai (Nobel Peace Prize Winner, 2007) and Mrs Pamela Mboya, widow of the late Tom Mboya (one time Kenyan representative to UN-Habitat); academicians, including Prof Philip Githinji (former vice chancellor, Kenyatta University) and Prof Geoffrey Maloiy (pioneer educationist and long serving professor at the University of Nairobi); top Kenyan journalists, including Hilary Ng'weno and Philip Ochieng'; as well as legislators such as Dr Adhu Awiti, and Kimani wa Nyoike.

Several other airlift beneficiaries became members of the cabinet or senior politicians and senior civil servants in the Government of Kenya. They include Arthur Magugu (former Minister for Finance), Samuel Onyango Ayodo (former Minister for Tourism) and Dr Zachary Onyonka (former Minister for Foreign Affairs). Others who benefited from the airlift included two former vice-presidents of Kenya, Dr Josephat Karanja and Prof George Saitoti.

It was during his stay in America that Obama Snr met his wife of the second marriage, Ann Dunham, later to become the mother of President

---

[3] David Remnick, *The Bridge*, p. 49.

Barack Obama. She was born in 1943, in Wichita, Kansas, to Stanley and Madelyn Dunham. Obama Snr had joined the University of Hawaii at Manoa in Honolulu in September 1959, becoming the first African foreign student at the university.

At the age of 23, Obama Snr had no inkling that, in a Russian language class, he would meet a cheerful 18 year old fresher who would define his posterity. The two began dating and after a brief courtship, were joined in matrimony – an act that in 1960 was a crime in most states. In many parts of the south, "My father could have been strung up from a tree for merely looking at my mother the wrong way," Barack Obama would later write. In keeping with Luo custom, they sought their parents' consent, who expressed doubts on the success of a mixed race marriage. The two went ahead and tied the knot.

Obama Snr's father, Hussein Onyango Obama, vehemently opposed the marriage, citing cultural incompatibility. He wrote his son, complaining: "How can you marry this white woman when you have responsibilities at home? Will this woman return with you and live as a Luo woman? Will she accept that you already have a wife and children? I have not heard of white people understanding such things. Their women are jealous and are used to being pampered."[4]

In the United States, colour bar was as rigorous as in apartheid South Africa. Everything was segregated – school, church, residence, train, bus, stadium, hotel, bar, restaurant, workplace, public toilet – everything. Inter-racial get-togethers between the sexes were strictly forbidden and heavily punishable. These legal restrictions were commonly flouted by young people, who regularly consorted, albeit discreetly. With the early collaboration that made possible the now epoch-making airlifts, many barriers were overcome.

In fact, it was only in Hawaii that interracial marriages were tolerated, while it was expressly forbidden in all other states. Hawaii is a melting pot of the Chinese, Japanese, Korean, Samoan, Filipino, and native islanders. Only African-Americans were not present in significant numbers.

---

[4] Barack Obama, *Dreams from My Father,* p. 422.

The Hawaiian Islands had become the fiftieth American state in August 1959. Neil Abercrombie found Hawaii almost like paradise, "... the smell of flowers was so rich as you walked down the street you thought the very atmosphere was perfumed."[5] Romantic liaisons between Caucasians and Africans gradually appeared.

From 1959 to 1960 Obama Snr had lived at the Charles H Atherton branch of the Young Men's Christian Association (YMCA) at 1810 University Avenue, which was just across the street from the university. And, from 1960 up until 1961, he lived in the Kaimuki neighbourhood, two miles southeast of the university at 625 11th Avenue.

Obama Snr married Stanley Ann Dunham in the Hawaiian island of Maui on 2 February 1961. Soon after their marriage they set up a new residence one mile (about 1.6 km) east of the university at 1482 Alencastre Street in the St Louis Heights neighbourhood. Six months after they wed, the couple were blessed with a baby boy – Barack Obama – who shared much more with his father than just the name. He was born on 4 August 1961 at the Kapi'olani Medical Centre for Women & Children in Honolulu, and his birth was announced in *The Honolulu Advertiser* and *The Honolulu Star-Bulletin*, listing his parents' address as 6085 Kalaniana'ole Highway in the Kuliouou neighbourhood of Honolulu, seven miles (about 11 km) east of the university – the rented home of Dunham's parents, Stanley and Madelyn Dunham.

At one time, there was a fake birth certificate claiming that President Obama had been born in Mombasa, Kenya. Of course that was quickly disproved. Commenting on that wild rumour, Leo Odera Omolo, a lifelong friend of Obama Snr, said: "Dr James Ang'awa, whose name appears in the certificate, was by then in charge of the Tuberculosis Unit at King George VI Hospital in Nairobi (now Kenyatta National Hospital), and could not have gone to Mombasa specifically to issue a birth certificate in a hospital where he did not work." Nevertheless President Obama finally closed that debate in April 2011 when he released his birth certificate to the public. The President admitted that he had been

---

[5] David Remnick, *The Bridge*, p. 51.

both amused and puzzled by the degree to which his place of birth had become an issue. "We do not have time for this kind of silliness. We've got better stuff to do," he told reporters.

While Ann Dunham dropped out of college after the birth of their son, Obama Snr continued with his education at the University of Hawaii in 1961 and 1962. He graduated from the University of Hawaii with a BA in Economics.

Soon after, in 1963 when his son was just two years old, Obama Snr left the family, ostensibly because his meagre stipend could not support the family if they lived together. He had earned his degree in economics in just three years, graduating in 1962. His performance earned him a scholarship to study at the prestigious Harvard University. President Barack Obama would later assert that racism on both sides of the family destroyed his parents' marriage. Ann's mother, who went by the nickname Tut, did not want a black son-in-law, and Obama Snr's father did not want "the Obama blood sullied by a white woman."[6]

Indeed, when Obama Snr finally returned to Kenya, the young Barack Obama and his mother stayed behind. The senior Obama had a mission: to return to his home country and help reinvent Kenya.

He may have wanted to take his new family with him, but he had a wife from a previous marriage back home, which complicated things somewhat. In any event, Ann decided not to follow him. She filed for divorce in Honolulu in January 1964, citing 'grievous mental suffering' – the reason given in most divorce cases at the time. Obama Snr signed the papers in Cambridge, Massachusetts, and did not contest the divorce. In due time, she remarried – to Lolo Soetoro, a Muslim official of the Director General's office in the Indonesian Army, who later became an oil company executive.

They later moved to Jakarta, Indonesia, where they – together with the young Barack Obama – would live for nearly five years. Ann and Lolo later bore a daughter, Maya Kassandra Soetoro-Ng. Through it all, she maintained contact with her first love. Another divorce would soon take

---

[6] Barack Obama, *Dreams from My Father*, p. 126.

place. By the time of her demise at the age of 52 in 1995, Ann Dunham, an economic anthropologist and rural development consultant, had not managed to revise her dissertation for publication, as she had planned.

Luckily, at the request of her daughter Maya Kassandra Soetoro-Ng, that task has now been completed for her by her fellow graduate student, Alice Dewey and Nancy Cooper, her graduate adviser. The resulting book, *Surviving Against the Odds*, reflects Dunham's commitment to helping small-scale village industries survive, her pragmatic approach to research and problem solving, and her impressive command of development policy. Her daughter, Maya Soetoro-Ng, has also released a book, *Ladder to the Moon*, which shares reminiscences of life with her late mother.

Another book on Ann Dunham, *A Singular Woman: The Untold Story of Barack Obama's Mother*, by Janny Scott, details her unconventional approach to things, but which greatly influenced her son, President Barack Obama.

Chapter 7

Life in Nairobi and Third Marriage

"It is not a lack of love, but a lack of friendship that makes unhappy marriages."
– Friedrich Wilhelm Nietzsche, a German philosopher, poet, cultural critic and classical philologist (1844-1900)

It was during his studentship at Harvard University that Obama Snr met Ruth Baker, later to become his wife of the third marriage. Ruth was a Jewish-American teacher, the daughter of prosperous Jewish-Lithuanian immigrants to the United States of America. Of all the four wives, Ruth is the one who stayed longest with Obama Snr. A close friend, Moses Wasonga, who was then a student in Boston, confirms that the two married shortly after they returned from the USA. The marriage certificate indicates that Barack Hussein Obama, aged 28, and Ruth Beatrice Baker, aged 27, married on 24 December 1964, at the District Commissioner's office in Nairobi. Ruth was the daughter of Maurice Joseph Baker, a salesman by profession and Ida Baker. Shortly after their return from the USA, the couple settled down in Nairobi together with Malik and Auma, the children from Obama Snr's first marriage. It is instructive that Obama senior was still married to his first wife Kezia when he married Ruth Baker.

Life in the Obama household was fun. Obama Snr then lived with Ruth, his wife by the third marriage, having divorced Ann Dunham. He had met her in Boston. The couple lived in Woodley Estate near Adams Arcade on Ngong Road, Nairobi. During that time, he had two children with Ruth – the first born son, Mark Okoth Obama and the last born son, David Opiyo Obama. Ezra, Obama Snr's cousin lived in the guest wing, a separate structure behind the main house.

Ezra Obama, a cousin of Obama Snr, is probably the one person alive who knows the adult Obama Snr best. "He was my cousin. He was older than I – much older, actually – by 15 years or so," he said in an interview. "I lived with him during my schooldays and after. At some stage in his life after he lost his job, he came along with his two children – his son Abong'o Malik Obama and his daughter, Auma Obama – to put up in my house as he sought to regain his bearings again."

In the early seventies, Ezra joined the Coca Cola Company. Obama Snr played a significant role in that opportunity since the General Manager, Godfrey Tetu, had been his close friend from their university days in the USA. He worked for Coca Cola from 1972 to the year 2000. He remains forever grateful to his cousin for that bit of assistance.

It was during the same period that Ruth worked at Nestlé Foods while Obama Snr was employed in the Ministry of Finance. Things seem to have picked up for the couple. He had bought a car, which he used to drop the children to school, and that Ruth would on occasion use when she was not dropped by the company car.

The household was very strict, Ezra recalls. "We would have dinner at exactly 6 pm," he says. "As an ambitious young executive, Obama Snr was often home late, but Ruth was always at hand. On the few occasions that Ruth would in her turn come home late, the houseboy, a lad named Obanda, would make sure that everything was in place. As a general rule, the children did their homework on time, and Ruth read with them. By and large, it was a normal, functional home." The house was ample, life comfortable, Ezra remembers. "The household employed the services of a house help, and a male servant. It was a three-bedroomed house that featured a master bedroom and two other bedrooms for the children."

Interestingly, Ezra describes Ruth as an extraordinarily big-hearted individual and a devoted wife to Obama Snr. "We did not find anything amiss (with her character) and I can answer for her because she raised me," he says with a gleam in his eye. "Ruth did not in any way discriminate against Malik or Auma, who were not her biological children. She treated every member of the household very well. I can vouch for this since we shared our meals on the same table."

During the school holidays, he would take the children to their village home in Nyang'oma K'Ogelo in Alego. They would cry to be shaved clean as was the custom among village children their age.

At around the same time, adds Ezra, Zeituni Abong'o – Obama Snr's sister – lived with the family for a short period while she attended school. Many other relatives would drop in frequently for visits, sometimes staying on as there was a spare room in the guest wing at the back of the house. But visitors also came from as far as the United States of America. At one time Ruth's parents visited from the USA and stayed with them for some time. During that visit, Obama Snr took his in-laws for a holiday at the coast. An American artist, Pake Zane, who was a student with Obama Snr at the University of Hawaii, also came for a visit. Ezra remembers how Pake Zane once prepared a delicious dish of meat with wine. It was a wonderful time.

The matrimonial relationship was cordial and mutually respectful, Ezra observes. "The two seemed deeply and genuinely in love. Whereas he would avoid open displays of affection, such as cuddling or kissing, especially when the children were around, one could still tell that the two were truly in love," he remarks. "He was very conscious of the fact that his children needed to be brought up differently from the way Americans brought up theirs."

Still, the couple had their fair share of disagreements, Ezra concedes. When that occurred, it would be readily apparent, especially to an adult who lived in the same house and shared the vicissitudes of life with the family. To calm nerves and bring down temperatures, Obama Snr would at such times come up with inventive diversions, such as taking the entire household out. Ruth and the children would joyfully frolic in the swimming pool, while Obama Snr would enjoy his choice of drinks on the terraces or in an adjoining restaurant. The family would return home cordial and relaxed, and the tension of the previous moment would naturally ease off.

Apparently, Ruth had no trouble adjusting to life as a woman and mother in an African household. She seemed so much at home in her new roles that Obama Snr must have educated her on African ways and more before she came to Africa. Like the quintessential African wife she had become, Ruth did not want anybody in the kitchen, traditionally the preserve of the woman of the house. She did all the cooking herself. She soon mastered the art of preparing the family's traditional dishes. She loved *ugali* (corn meal), the staple dish in Kenya.

"In the year 1971," Amir Otieno, a half-brother to Obama Snr, picks up the story, "After I had completed secondary school at Nyabondo High School, I went to visit him at his residence in Woodley Estate, Nairobi. I met the whole family, including Ruth, and their two children – Roy, who is now called Malik, and Rita Auma. I stayed in Nairobi during the period 1972-1974.

"They lived a comfortable life then," he adds wistfully. "During that period the family employed a lady called Juliana as a house help. His cousin Ezra also stayed with them."

"Obama Snr was a man of few words. When he came home, he would enquire whether the children had eaten, and if there was any problem. Ruth was at that time employed by Nestlé. Following Ruth's gracious intervention, I got a temporary employment position with the same company," Amir relates. "The atmosphere at home was very good. There were no quarrels that I can remember," he concludes.

Razik, the other son of Habiba by her second marriage, expressed the same sentiments, which were echoed by Mama Zarifa, the last born in Habiba's household (now deceased).

Eventually, however, this promising interracial marriage ended in divorce. For Ezra, that was an eventuality straight out of the blue. There were no indications of any serious underlying tension or disagreement, no warning signs. All had seemed placid, save for the occasional tiff that is to be found in any normal household. Even though it has been reported variously that Obama Snr administered beatings on his wife, Ruth, Ezra says that he never witnessed any such incident for the time that he lived together with the Obamas.

According to Ezra, it is not quite clear why the couple divorced since there was no obvious contention or violent confrontation. Still, it is interesting that the divorce occurred after Obama Snr had lost his job and, as a result, the family was undergoing some level of financial difficulty. Obama Snr's loss of employment was devastating to his social standing. With the demands of his young family, coupled with wider responsibilities of the African extended family, his waning financial status soon got the better of him. It was only a matter of time before his wife of the third marriage deserted him, blaming it on domestic violence. Following the divorce, she took her two children with her, and settled with her new husband, Simeon Ndesandjo who, incidentally, had been a close family friend and a regular visitor to the Obama household. The children were given the name of their stepfather, discarding their biological father's name, a move that greatly infuriated Obama Snr.

The family had acquired property off Convent Drive in the Lavington area of Nairobi. They had also bought a house on Chalbi Street. During the divorce, Ruth claimed the latter property for the children's upkeep, but Obama Snr complained that he did not want to lose the house. Available documents indicate that they divorced on 15 March 1972 at the High Court in Nairobi.

After she had left, Ruth invited Ezra and his wife for lunch in her new house on Rhapta Road in Westlands, Nairobi. Then, she lived alone and had not remarried. Fortunately, the lady who had served as her house help during her former marriage had moved with her. They served a delicious fare of fish and *ugali* that the visitors greatly enjoyed. Half in jest, Ezra challenged her to come back to her husband. He was explicitly rebuffed.

After divorcing Obama Snr, Ruth married a Kenyan of Tanzanian origin, Ndesandjo. One of her sons by Obama Snr, Mark Okoth Obama Ndesandjo, is author of the book, *Nairobi to Shenzhen*.[1] A businessman and musician, he has lived in southern China for many years. When his parents divorced, his family repudiated the Obama name for that of his

---

[1] Mark Okoth Ndesandjo Obama, *Nairobi to Shenzhen*, 2010.

adoptive father, Ndesandjo. "I didn't have positive memories of my dad because of domestic violence," he said. His father was brilliant, says Mark, but alcoholism drove him to beat his wife and children.

"I am an Obama, and a large part of my life was a repudiation of that," he told *Time*. "To a certain extent, my brother (President Obama) … opened my eyes to things that I had left behind for a long time." Indeed, when he watched the televised scenes of joy in Chicago's Grant Park on the night a man with that hated last name was declared president of the United States, his perspective changed. "There was this remarkable movement from fear towards hope," he says. "I was so proud of my brother Barack."[2] He has now reclaimed his original surname, Obama, and added Okoth, a name common among his father's Luo people that means 'of the rain'.

---

[2] http://www.time.com/time/world/article/0,8599,1939695,00.html.

Chapter 8

Last Marriage, Challenges and Demise

"May a man live well enough and long enough, to leave many joyful widows behind him"
– Roman Payne, American-born novelist and poet

A diligent and generous man, Tom Mboya was a true nationalist and Pan-Africanist. His undeniable charisma and gift of the garb earned him worldwide recognition and respect. He made an immortal contribution to black African empowerment in Kenya through the airlift project. In life, Mboya was many things to many people. A lot has been accredited to him. He was a brilliant and charismatic leader, a renowned trade unionist, an astute politician and a statesman. He was a self-made man who, to the very end of his life, remained committed to the total liberation of Africans both at home and in the diaspora. He placed great value on education and, having missed the direct route, pursued further education through correspondence. He enrolled at the Efficiency Correspondence College of South Africa, majoring in economics.

Tom Mboya, the architect of the famous airlifts was also one of Obama Snr's mentors. His sudden death was to have catastrophic effects on the life and career of his protégé.

* * *

On Saturday 5 July 1969, Obama Snr went to Nairobi's Government Road (now Moi Avenue), with a companion, Mrs Kinyengi. There he spotted Mboya's car get into the parking lot. Tom Mboya was by then a cabinet minister in the Kenya government while Obama Snr was a senior economist in the same government. Obama Snr saw Mboya get out of the car and the two were soon engaged in friendly banter. "You are parked on a yellow line, you will get a ticket," he jokingly told Mboya, who laughed it off. He introduced his companion to Mboya and the two chatted for a while before Mboya went into Chhani's Pharmacy, located in a building which is now the site of Norwich Union Towers. After serving him, the pharmacist, Mohini Sehmi, walked him to the door. All of a sudden, several gun shots rang out and Tom Mboya fell down in a pool of blood. As fate would have it, Obama Snr witnessed the assassination of Tom Mboya at a close range and was among the last people to talk to him before his demise. As a key witness of the assassination, Obama Snr was to testify in the murder trial that followed.[1]

One of the most difficult moments of Kenya's political history followed the assassination of the flamboyant politician. Tom Mboya was shot dead on the fateful morning of 5 July 1969. Weeks later, a 30-year old mechanic was arrested and charged with the murder. Obama Snr made a bold decision to testify in the controversial trial that followed the assassination, a decision that may have played a large part in tipping the scales against him.

As was expected, Mboya's burial on Rusinga Island was marked by palpable tension and high rhetoric among the political leaders who attended the ceremony. Since it was widely believed that members of the ruling ethnic Kikuyu elite of the time were involved in his death, not many dared attend the burial.

Only J M Kariuki – later to be assassinated – and Mwai Kibaki, later to become president, were the top government leaders of Kikuyu ethnic origin that attended. In his autobiography, Njenga Karume gives his version of the events that followed and in particular the oath-taking by the Kikuyu community that was administered in the president's backyard of Gatundu and all over Central Kenya.[2]

www He was then a senior economist with the Ministry of Planning and Finance. He rubbed the government officials the wrong way

---

[1] "Mboya case witness flies in", *Daily Nation,* 8 September 1969.

[2] Njenga Karume, *Beyond Expectations: From Charcoal to Gold,* p. 205.

when, after the Minister for Economic Planning and Development was assassinated, he angrily demanded an explanation on his death. An incensed official immediately handed him the sack.[3]

According to at least one friend, he subsequently became convinced that he had been targeted for assassination after his testimony. He said he had been hit by a car not long after and left for dead," said Pake Zane, who attended the University of Hawaii with Obama Snr. "He did not say specifically who had done it, but he said it was the same people who had killed Mboya."[4]

"His testimony was the nail in the coffin," said Caroline Elkins, an associate professor of African Studies at Harvard University. "He probably made the right calculation. His mentor was gone. His career was probably over. So, why not do the right thing and testify? He had no one to protect him either way. So it was a very bold move."[5]

During a visit from one of his old school friend, Zane, in 1974, Obama confided that he had seen Mboya's killer and claimed to be the only witness who could identify him. According to Tom Mboya's biography, *Tom Mboya: The Man Kenya Wanted to Forget,* nine eye-witnesses to the shooting failed to identify the suspect in a police lineup.

Tom Mboya's widow, Pamela Mboya, did not wish to discuss her husband's death either. Several historians of the period, however, believe that Obama may have held on to his secret for good reason. "Foes of the powers-that-be in Kenya are prone to be eliminated," said Cohen.[6]

---

[3] Joe Ombuor, *the East African Standard*, 4 November 2008.

[4] Sally Jacobs, *"A Father's Charm, Absence"*, *Boston Globe*, 21 September 2008, Available at:http://www.boston.com/news/politics/2008/articles/2008/09/21/a_fathers_charm_absence/ (Accessed: 4 January 2014).

[5] Sally Jacobs, *"A Father's Charm, Absence"*, *Boston Globe*, 21 September 2008, Available at:http://www.boston.com/news/politics/2008/articles/2008/09/21/a_fathers_charm_absence/ (Accessed 4 January 2014).

[6] Sally Jacobs, *"A Father's Charm, Absence"*, *Boston Globe*, 21 September 2008, Available at:http://www.boston.com/news/politics/2008/articles/2008/09/21/a_fathers_charm_absence/ (Accessed 4 January 2014).

The events that followed were not particularly good for Obama Snr. At one time, Ezra, his cousin, relates, "Obama Snr was thrown out of his residential house at Nairobi's Woodley Estate for failing to pay rent. He was jobless at the time. This was a very disastrous time. He had issued a rent cheque that did not go through. His landlords, the Nairobi City Council, came and bundled everybody out of the house."

* * *

Ezra had now moved into his own house at Ngara flats on the other side of town. When Obama Snr was evicted from his house due to non-payment of rent, he was forced to move to Ezra's house.

"He came with what remained of his family – his son Malik and daughter Auma – since his wife Ruth had left with the other two children," relates Ezra. "They stayed on for about four to five months. In those days, he would spend most of his time at Dr Oluoch's place – Chandlane Nursing Home." That Ezra, who was partly raised by Obama Snr, later came to his rescue is a commendable state of affairs best captured in the Luo saying, *chien kiyany* ('never despise your past').

Obama Snr had walked a tightrope over the years and found it difficult to maintain a balanced life during his short tenure in employment. His working life suffered setbacks due to the politics of the day that put both family and social demands at the crossroads. His daughter, Auma Obama, says her father had become a victim of the clash between the Africa Luo and the Western cultures and the expectations that had been so heavily placed on his shoulders. With rapid westernisation in the community, it was a struggle to imbibe the best of the new world while keeping the best of the old world, which was a real struggle as the worlds themselves seemed incompatible and at war.

Due to the frosty political environment, Obama Snr remained out of employment for a long time. Eventually, as his long-time friend and former diplomat, Caleb Omogi, explained, he bumped into Mwai Kibaki, a former Minister for Finance, later to become vice-president and president of Kenya. It was Kibaki who helped Obama Snr get employment at the Treasury once again. Both Kibaki and Obama Snr knew each other well and were both former employees of Shell Oil Company. They bumped into each other at a social club in Nairobi.

"What drink can I offer you?" Mwai Kibaki asked him.

"A double whisky," he replied.

"And what will you take it with?" Kibaki inquired further.

"Another double whisky!" he bellowed back.

This response puzzled Kibaki.

Since whisky is a highly concentrated alcoholic drink, it is common practice for consumers to mix it with a soda or any other mild drink.

"I cannot offer you a drink myself because I don't have a job," Obama Snr explained.

"We have to get you a job, you just can't stay without a job," Kibaki told him.

After some pleasantries, Kibaki gave him an appointment for the following morning.

He kept the appointment – and reported straight to work. As a planning economist, it was not a dream job, considering his credentials. But it came at the right time and helped him pick up his life once again.

That was in 1981, when he again took up service as principal economist in the Ministry of Economic Planning and Finance. He was assigned to head the industrial development department.

During his leadership of the department, he represented Kenya at numerous regional and international conferences that discussed a wide range of issues. One of his favourite subjects was the economic integration of the East African states and the African continent.

"I can say with some authority that his life was whole again," concludes Ezra. "After losing his wife Ruth, he met and married Jael Atieno from Kano in Kenya's Nyanza region, with whom they later had a son. By the time of his death, he had a functional family, was in employment, and lived in a decent government house in Upper Hill, Nairobi. His life was back on track again."

* * *

Barack Obama Snr met Jael Atieno, his wife by the fourth marriage, through his sister when the two girls were still students together at Khalsa Girls Secondary School in Nairobi. Jael then lived with her elder sister Janet, who was Obama Snr's neighbour. Their courtship was stormy. Janet objected to it on the grounds that her sister was too young to get married at that time. In any case, Jael was still in school and Janet was responsible for paying her school fees. At one moment, Janet literally stormed Obama Snr's house in an effort to prevent the burgeoning romance. She was shocked to find her younger sister comfortably entrenched in the house. Unperturbed, Jael confidently told her sister that she was happily married. She came in a second time, with the same results.

If anyone could throw some light on the latter years of the mature Obama Snr, it is his wife of the fourth and last marriage, Jael Atieno. It was with her that he lived out his last and final years, up to the very day of his disappearance and his subsequent death. So, when Jael Atieno Obama, now Jael Dixon, visited Nairobi in the latter part of September 2010, she was interviewed by Julius Opiyo. What follows is her story.

When Jael first met Obama Snr at her sister Janet Anyango's house in Nairobi's Madaraka Estate in 1981, he had long divorced his previous wife, Ruth. Earlier on, Barack Obama Snr had known Jael's sister, Janet, who worked at the American Embassy. The two had become good friends. Never one to mince his words, he was struck with the beauty of Jael when they first met, and he did not keep quiet about it.

"Oh Janet, is this your sister?" he asked.

"She is my younger sister," Janet replied.

"She is so beautiful!"

"She goes to school and helps me take care of the house in the evenings and weekends."

"She is a very smart and fastidious girl, and I really appreciate that."

After that, the two did not meet again for quite a while. Then, one fine afternoon, Jael says, Obama Snr's sister, Masat Osumba, who was also her schoolmate, invited her over for a visit. He chanced by and found the two in the house.

"Aren't you Janet's sister?" he asked her. She nodded in the affirmative. He then just told her that she was welcome.

The two girls were good friends and regularly visited each other during the weekends. They lived in adjacent estates – Jael and her sister lived in Madaraka, while Obama Snr lived in Mawenzi Gardens.

One day, Obama Snr just blurted out to his sister, Masat, that he wanted to marry Jael. It was hard to tell whether he meant it, or it was just a joke. Still, she repeated the conversation to Jael, who poured cold water on it.

"Me, marry an old man? Never!"

That seemed to mark the end of the matter, but not for long. The two girls continued visiting each other and Obama Snr got more and more interested in Jael. Then, one day, "It just happened," says Jael. Around the same time, Janet lost her job, and Jael's education was suddenly in doubt. Obama Snr offered to take her through school, and that was arranged. Things got thicker after that.

The couple was soon expecting. When Jael got pregnant in 1981, Obama Snr was extremely supportive. Obama Snr would lovingly caress Jael's bulging tummy, proclaiming that they were soon to deliver his father, Hussein Onyango Obama. He was referring to the common practice among African communities of naming the firstborn sons after their grandfather.

He insisted that the baby would be a boy and proudly declared that he would be named after both his father and his brother George Were.

True to his prediction, she delivered a healthy baby boy, who was given the composite name, George Hussein Obama. Born only six months before his demise, George was to be the last born child of Obama Snr.

When Rita Auma came visiting from Germany, she brought some presents for the boy. David Opiyo also lived with the family for a time, before he went and lived with his brother, Malik. He much preferred to stay like that and did not really spend much time with his mother, Ruth. He stayed on until Jael delivered George.

He really loved the youngster, and would always encourage him saying, "I will support you"; "I will help you". He continued doing that even after the death of Obama Snr. George had the same generous streak that Obama Snr had.

"If you asked Obama Snr for money to buy food and he didn't have it, he would feel very bad about it," said Jael. "Don't worry," he would say. "I will get some money from the bank. The children have to eat."

Obama Snr was a very jovial man, says Jael. "He loved his children too, except that they often misunderstood him." Sometimes, the children would come along and ask for pocket money. One day, Mark came along with David, but apparently, Mark refused to enter the house. So Jael went and asked Obama Snr to talk to him. But he did not, saying that he would not force Mark or any of the children to come to him. It would appear that Mark had somehow grown distant from his father.

Obama Snr's biological mother, Habiba Akumu *nyar* Njoga, also visited the family. She came almost immediately the two started living together. When Jael was three months pregnant, he took her to visit Habiba upcountry. After sharing a meal with her, the couple proceeded to Kendu Bay to meet the other members of his family. They spent the night and, the following day, proceeded to Alego K'Ogelo.

* * *

Whereas Obama Snr was able to secure employment in his final years, his life was plagued by several accidents, recalls Rev Nick Ajuoga. "His drinking habits were what probably made him so prone to accidents," Nick Ajuoga related. "I would imagine so, because he was having these accidents at very odd times of the night after he had had a few drinks, obviously."

Obama Snr loved his bottle, concedes Ezra, but only as much as the next man. "I never saw him come home staggering," he says, denying that Obama Snr drank too much. But yes, he had several accidents in his lifetime, he concedes. "I remember one or two; I especially remember one accident on Ngong Road that occurred near the Impala Club, around Harlequins. I actually took him to Kenyatta National Hospital myself. The other driver was a white man."

It was a serious accident. "He broke an arm and a leg," narrates Ezra. "That was in the late 1970s – around '78 or '79. He stayed in hospital for about three months. It took a while for him to completely recuperate, but he was finally able to walk and even drive."

The last and fatal accident he had was especially terrible – and mysterious. "I was living in Madaraka Estate while he lived in Mawenzi Gardens, just next door so we were able to see each other every other day," Ezra relates. "The accident occurred on Kilimanjaro Road, and it took us several days to find out. His wife, Jael Atieno, called me inquiring about his whereabouts, since he had not been seen at home lately. We started looking for him.

Mwana Hawa, the only surviving sister of Obama Snr also gave her own version of the story. "We had a relative named Sammy who had died in Nairobi," Mwana Hawa narrates how the family received news of his passage. "Some close relatives had gone to collect his body from the City Mortuary. That is when they saw Obama Snr's body lying there. I was with my mother Habiba Akumu *nyar* Njoga, when the sad news reached home. She screamed and collapsed," Mwana Hawa related.

"At that time, he had just arrived from abroad," Mwana Hawa continues. "He had left home, saying that he was reporting to work. He actually went to the office, but never returned home. After two days, his now thoroughly worried wife started looking for him. Not finding him at work, he went to report the matter at the Police Station, where she found his car in the police yard."

* * *

Three days before he died, Barack Obama Snr kept talking about his imminent death. He repeatedly told Jael that in case he died, she should ensure that all his children inherited part of his estate. On his last day home, he came in and sat on the couch. After taking the meal that Jael offered, he invited her to sit with him and told her his last wishes.

"When I die, some people will come to fight you," he said ominously to Jael.

"In fact, tomorrow I am going to prepare a will," he added.

When Jael enquired on his sudden preoccupation with his own death, his reply was simple: He knew when things were not right.

"If I die before George is 18 years," he continued, "ensure that there is a trust for him. I want him to get the best possible education, just like my other children.

"If I die, make sure all my children, including Barry, are made aware of it immediately."

"But Barry is in the USA!" Jael protested.

"If I die, just go to the Ministry of Foreign Affairs and tell them to contact Ambassador Noah Okulo in Saudi Arabia, he will then contact the USA ambassador and they will look for him. If not, Ambassador Morris Omuony in Germany can do the same. Just make sure that Barry knows that I am dead."

Still, his sudden demise was a great shock for Jael. For two days, nobody knew his whereabouts. The last time he was in the house, he had left to buy some detergent at Nairobi West shopping centre. He never came back. There was a curfew on following the abortive military coup of August 1982, so Jael initially thought his return had been prevented by the police. This trend was worrying because there were some mysterious deaths around the same time, particularly among the Luo people, who were perceived to have supported the attempted coup.

On the third day, Jael felt the first signs of unease. She started looking for him. She went first to his office and inquired of his secretary, Naomi. He had not been seen in the office for two days, when he had last left to attend a government meeting at Wilson Airport, where he was scheduled to meet some Japanese officials and take them to Nyali Beach, Mombasa.

Next, she inquired of his best friend, James Otieno, who had an office on the 8th floor of the same building. He too had not seen his friend for a while. He suggested that Jael check at Kenyatta National Hospital casualty department for any reported cases of injured patients or new admissions over the last two days. On the way to the hospital, Jael relates, she had this very strong feeling to stop at Nairobi's traffic police headquarters, just adjacent to the hospital, for inquiries. Immediately she entered the police compound, she saw Obama Snr's car. With mounting dread, she accosted the first policeman she encountered.

"Where is the owner of that car," she demanded, pointing at Obama Snr's car.

"He is gone," the policeman replied nonchalantly.

"What do you mean, gone? Where has he gone?" Jael asked angrily.

With tears welling up in her eyes, she pushed blindly on into the police reception area, where she hoped to get some clear answers. The policeman on duty asked her whether she was a relation to the owner of the car.

"I am his wife," she answered simply.

At that moment, she was directed to another officer inside the station. He asked her to get another relative to accompany her, and he would show them to the present whereabouts of the car's owner.

"I felt so tired and weak," Jael related. "Suddenly my feet felt numb and heavy, so I removed my shoes and carried them. When one of my neighbours, Mr Alila, saw me and asked why I was carrying my shoes, I burst out crying."

Both Alila and his wife agreed to accompany her back to the police station straightaway. At the police station, the officer gave them a note to take to the City Mortuary to identify the body. According to the post-mortem report, Obama Snr had died from internal bleeding following extensive internal injuries. "Still," reports Mwana Hawa, "we found it strange that he had driven past the gate. Apparently, the accident had occurred hardly 300 metres from his house. The Police report indicated that he had hit an electricity pole, but we couldn't verify that because the vehicle had been towed away."

The Police, added Mwana Hawa, told her they had found him in his car, dead. "The car was a Chevrolet registration number KTH 018, which he had bought while still at the Treasury," she asserts. "But his body had no visible injuries. They had taken his body to the City Mortuary," she concludes. His cousin Elijah K'Obilo, who then worked as a salesman for General Motors in Nairobi had sold him the car.

"As a family, we entertained some doubts about the official version of events, but had no recourse," Ezra concludes. It is such inexplicable circumstances that were to fuel suspicions of foul play that have yet to be conclusively laid to rest.

* * *

Following his demise, Obama Snr was accorded a Christian burial after observing some key components of Luo traditional ceremonies such as *tero buru*. Earlier on, there had been a standoff as to whether the late should be accorded a Christian or a Muslim burial. Mama Sarah relates that her attempts to insist on a Muslim burial were overwhelmed by relatives' and government demands that the late Obama Snr be given a Christian burial.

Unfortunately, Obama Snr died before he could formalise his marriage to Jael. He had promised her parents that he would bring the dowry in a ceremony to take place in December, but he died in November. The delay was mainly on account of her pregnancy since, according to Luo custom, it was not permissible for the ceremony to take place while she was pregnant. The couple had only lived together for one and a half years.

In the aftermath of Obama Snr's funeral, Jael was absorbed in the Ministry of Finance and Economic Planning. She lived alone in Nairobi for some time before she got involved in a nine-year relationship with a Frenchman, Christian Bertrand, who was by then working in Nairobi. Towards the end of that period, she travelled to Korea where she met her current husband, Hosea Dixon, who then served with the USA army in Korea. The two got married and later relocated to the USA. Jael feels proud that her late husband's dream that the junior Obama would be a great man had been fulfilled in her own lifetime.

She currently lives in the USA state of Georgia with her husband, Hosea Dixon, an African-American.[7]

Her son George Obama, the step-brother to US President Barack Obama, is author of the biography, *Homeland* (co-authored with Damien Lewis).[8] The book tells how, in his later life, he dropped out of school and drifted into neighbourhood gangs. He ended up in prison, from where he came out as organiser for the rights and dignity of prisoners.

---

[7] George Obama (with Damien Lewis), *Homeland* pp. 20 and 236.

[8] George Obama (with Damien Lewis), *Homeland,* St Martin's Press, New York, 2009.

Chapter 9

Short Distinguished Career: A Balancing Act

"My father became a victim of the clash between the Kenyan Luo and the Western cultures and the expectations that had been so heavily placed on his shoulders."
—Auma Obama

Blessed with rare intellect and driving ambition, Obama Snr was a brilliant individual with a promising career. Following his return from the USA, he was expected to teach at a university to maintain his sponsorship for completing his PhD. He is said to have served a short stint at Makerere University in Kampala, Uganda. He soon left and joined the University of Nairobi, where he also served briefly as a part-time lecturer. Apparently, that was not enough to attract the sponsorship. He was told to get a full-time job at the university, which did not materialise. His subsequent employment in non-academic institutions meant that he was no longer eligible for the doctoral sponsorship.

Terry Ryan, a long time professor at the University of Nairobi and later on Director of Planning in the Ministry of Planning, Government of Kenya, recollects meeting him at the University of Nairobi:

> *I was working at the University of Nairobi. He must have come back from the United States because my recollection is seeing him coming to the department at the University and taking up a teaching position. He was employed there for a very short time. I can remember his office and everything like that because he too then went into civil service. That's my recollection. He was there in the economics department, at least for some time. That would be in the mid to late sixties.*

Obama Snr joined Shell Company on 11 August 1964 and worked there until 31 July 1966. He was employed as a management trainee in the finance department. According to records available at Shell offices in Nairobi, he held a B.A. (Economics) degree from the University of Hawaii awarded in 1962, and an M.A. (Economics) degree from Harvard University. According to Mwaura M Ngaari, the external affairs manager at Shell Kenya, his personal file indicated that he was a PhD pursuant at Harvard University. By the time he left the organisation, he was head of management accounts. Throughout this time, his office was at Shell BP House, Harambee Avenue, Nairobi. The building has since been acquired by the government and was the office of the former Prime Minister, Raila Odinga and later the Deputy President's office.

After his return from the USA, he lived in Nairobi for most of his adult life. Immediately after his homecoming, he first stayed at Rosslyn Gardens before moving to Woodley Estate in Nairobi.

He subsequently moved to Ngara Flats where he stayed for a short while with his cousin, Ezra Obama, while he was out of a job. On regaining employment, he moved to the government quarters at Kariokor and finally to Mawenzi Gardens Estate in the Upper Hill area of Nairobi.

Rev Nick Ajuoga, who was both Obama Snr's neighbour and colleague at work, confirms his tenure at Shell.

"I knew Obama Snr well after his return from the USA," he says. "He had come home and was engaged to work with Shell Oil Company. I was also working for Shell at that time."

"He worked for Shell for about two years. The local boss, Alan Ross, was very meticulous. For Obama to work for them that long, (it) means he was diligent," adds Ajuoga. "When the time for him to leave came, he informed us that he had got greener pastures and wanted to move on to the next job," Ajuoga concludes.

According to Dr Francis Masakhalia, he next served in a senior position in the research department at the Central Bank of Kenya (CBK). The leadership of the bank had just been Africanised, and Duncan Ndegwa had taken over as Governor after relinquishing his position as Head of the Public Service and Secretary to the Cabinet. Expatriates at that time were the dominant officers in CBK technical departments. One needed tact to work with Ndegwa and the expatriate team, but Obama Snr, a bright and rather arrogant person, was rather lacking in that trait. In addition, he was involved in several motor accidents while serving with the bank, which led to hospitalisation going into months. This partly explains why he faced problems with his employers at the Central Bank.

Thereafter, he took up service with the Kenya Tourism Development Corporation (KTDC) in 1969 as a Senior Development Officer. However, the loss of his position at the Central Bank took a heavy toll on his morale, and he was never at his best again. Still, according to Francis Masakhalia, he made great contributions to the design of the strategy for the development of tourist circuits, hotels and game lodges.

He also served a short stint at the Ministry of Planning and Finance – the Treasury – of the Government of Kenya. However, his enemies connived to frustrate his work at the ministry. "He was shuffled between desks, which accorded him little time to settle down and get the job done," said Prof Terry Ryan, who shared an office with him at the time.

Due to the polarised political situation that obtained at the time, Obama Snr found it hard to access opportunities and settle down to his professional calling. His entire working life was marked with increasing frustration and dashed hopes.

It may soon be possible to see Obama Snr on TV or video. He hosted a weekly television talk show, *Wheels of progress,* during the late 1960s, where he engaged various personalities in discussing economic issues affecting the country and the society. The programme was screened on the government-owned *Voice of Kenya* television (now Kenya Broadcasting Corporation – KBC). Members of the Obama family are negotiating with KBC to release the video tapes to the Obama Opiyo Foundation.

* * *

Obama Snr may have had a short and chequered working life, but it was still eventful. In February 1970, he addressed an African business people's seminar at the Kenya Polytechnic, Nairobi, which was attended by members of the emerging business community. In line with the government policy of economic independence, he encouraged them to direct their efforts to trade as opposed to farming, which was their major preoccupation in the period before and after independence.[1]

On 4 March 1970, while yet at KTDC, Obama Snr participated in the monthly meeting of the Executive Committee of the East African Hotelkeepers' Association that was addressed by Assistant Minister for Tourism and Wildlife, J M Kariuki, who was later assassinated. The issue of indigenisation of the economy arose. "We are very concerned at the reluctance of some of you to train Africans for responsible positions in the hotel industry," the Minister told the largely expatriate audience. In defence, the association said that for more than eight years, they had been trying to get a training scheme off the ground and had achieved some success in the junior cadres of the trade. It had also forwarded further recommendations to the Minister.[2]

After visiting his son in Hawaii in 1972, Obama Snr stopped over in Boston where he attended a party hosted by the Kenyan community there. He met many prominent Kenyan students, among them Prof Peter Kenya. "We met in his brother's apartment on 17th Perry Street in Cambridge, Massachusetts," Prof Kenya reported. "His brother had hosted a party in honour of Kenyan students in the USA." He encouraged them to study and pursue their highest potential. He also talked highly about his son.

Just before his unexpected demise in 2009, Prof Peter Kenya, a professor at Kenyatta University Department of Environmental Studies and Community Development, reported a subsequent meeting they had in the USA in 1977.

That time, Obama Snr had accompanied the Kenyan ambassador in the USA and other government officials who had come to woo members of the Kenyan community there to return home and help build the fledgling nation. Then, in 1978, he represented Kenya at an international conference on the managerial implications of transfer of technology from developed to developing countries in Seoul, South Korea. In October 1979, Obama

---

[1] *Daily Nation*, 10 February 1970.
[2] *Daily Nation*, 10 March 1970.

Snr joined a high-powered delegation of government officials from Kenya, Uganda, Tanzania and Zambia that flew to New York for talks with representatives of the South and East Africa United States Conference Lines. The talks covered proposals for harmonisation of freight charges and the removal of bottlenecks to trade.[3]

In July 1980, he headed a Kenya government delegation to Ethiopia for negotiations that were meant to pave the way for a regional multi-sectoral investigation and study covering water resources, wildlife management, fisheries, tourism, agriculture, forestry, and social and basic infrastructure to be funded by the then European Economic Community (EEC).[4]

J F Oling'a, who joined the Ministry of Finance in 1981 and served briefly with Obama Snr, vividly recalls the few moments they shared together. "As an economist," he reports, "Obama Snr may have been involved in the formulation of Kenya's monetary policy papers as well as the East African Currency Board."

"Having been among the first people from his village to earn a university degree," adds Paul Onyango 'Maji', "Obama Snr became a champion of education at the local level." According to Mama Sarah, he helped organise harambees (voluntary community fund-raisers) for the construction of Nyang'oma Secondary School. He also supported similar fund-raisers for the upgrading of Nyang'oma Primary School as well as the local health centre. Following his death, the secondary school collapsed and was only revived through the efforts of one *Mzee* Nyagude.

---

[3] *Daily Nation*, 13 October 1979.
[4] *Daily Nation*, 2 July 1980.

Chapter 10

Obamanomics: Vision for Kenya

"We can have a high rate of growth economically and yet not develop economically, politically and socially."
– Barack Obama Snr

The nascent ideology of Barack Obama Snr may be understood from perhaps one of his best scripts, his critique of the government's seminal Sessional Paper No. 10 of 1965 that was titled: "African Socialism and its Application to Planning in Kenya". As William Cohen and E S Atieno Odhiambo explain in their book, *The Risks of Knowledge*[1], he wrote the paper in response to the 'mixed economy' blueprint that sought to combine a version of liberal capitalism necessary to attract foreign capital with elements of domestic socialism as the most equitable way of distributing the anticipated economic gains of independence. His critique, which appeared in the *East African Journal* in 1965, was titled, *"Problems Facing our Socialism."*[2]

Obama Snr had studied economics at Harvard University and was then in Nairobi, working on his doctorate. His dissertation was on the topic, "An econometric model of the stable theory development." His was one of the critiques picked among the many received in the journal office of the Ministry of Planning that drafted Sessional Paper No. 10 on African socialism. When the government released the policy paper, Kenya had attained full independence two years earlier from British colonial rule.

---

[1] William Cohen and ES Atieno Odhiambo, *The Risks of Knowledge: Investigations into the Death of the Hon Minister John Robert Ouko in Kenya, 1990.*

[2] Barack Obama Snr, *Problems Facing our Socialism,* Available at: http://www.politico.com/static/PPM41_eastafrica.html (Accesed 10 July 2009).

The government stated in the document that, under colonialism, the people of Kenya had no voice in government; the nation's natural resources were organised and developed mainly for the benefit of non-Africans. In this context, the government indicated that the nation's human resources remained largely uneducated, untrained, inexperienced and un-benefited by the growth of the economy. With independence therefore, Kenya intended to mobilise its resources to attain a rapid rate of economic growth for the benefit of its people. The government paper further stated that the major economic mobilisation and reorganisation of resources that the transitions implied could not be realised without planning, direction, control and cooperation. It was thus important to note that planning and direction implied objectives and mechanisms. Kenyans were bound to ask themselves where they were going and how they would get there. It is for the purposes of answering these questions that the paper was prepared. The paper went further to deal with matters of policy.

As a fresh graduate from Harvard, Obama Snr clearly demonstrated that he was keen to put his much-needed expertise to practice in the service of his newly independent country. It was in this context that he made his mind known on the policies that were to have far reaching effects on the young African nation.

In his rejoinder, Obama Snr congratulated the Kenyan government for its bold step in articulating its aspirations. Then he went ahead to respond to the various components of the document. Although the paper outlined the government's intentions, he contended, it was not clear if the Kenyan version of socialism was in tandem with 'African Socialism' as purveyed elsewhere on the continent since both remained vaguely defined. The desire for independence from other countries was laudable, he admitted, but for as long as it was not made clear how that would be achieved – both politically and economically – it rang hollow. As an economist, he must have foreseen that a clearly political alignment was necessary if the economic direction indicated was to bear fruit.

* * *

In the paper, the government proclaimed its adoption of a non-alignment policy. This was in the context of the bipolar politics of the time that pitted the capitalist West led by the USA against the Socialist Eastern bloc, led by the USSR. The non-alignment policy adopted was positive, Obama Snr noted, but it was not accompanied by a road map for implementation. This resulted in lack of commitment to firm relations. While the emerging states rolled out their ideologies, the undefined 'African Socialism' stated its independence from 'foreign ideologies' without clarifying the foreign ideology being referred to. Other than merely stating its independence, it appears to have failed to define its relationship with other countries, he argued. It is clear from the onset that Obama Snr had detected nascent loopholes in the political structure of the country that could be detrimental to the building of the young nation's economy.

On the subject of the application of African Socialism to planning in Kenya, he felt that too much emphasis was being put on economic growth, which could be to the detriment of other objectives. Kenyans should rather be more concerned with economic development, which is richer and more relevant, he argued. "We can have a high rate of growth economically and yet not develop both economically, politically and socially," Obama Snr noted. This would imply that he was more concerned with building the local infrastructure and human resource base that would define the country's future.

* * *

On the critical question of foreign exchange, the paper made its opinion known and stated in part: "At the present time, Kenya is succeeding in borrowing enough from abroad to pay for its excess of imports over exports. Kenya does not now have a foreign exchange problem, but great care must be exercised to ensure that the steps we take to promote development, including our foreign policy, do not create this problem." In response, Obama Snr proposed that a form of import licensing be introduced which would look at the imported goods in terms of their contribution to growth and development, unless they were things that were not produced locally. He clearly demonstrated his deep concern

77

for the welfare of the populace and the need to augment their ability to afford the basic necessities.

"We should take measures to encourage more import-substituting industries and have selective controls with high preference being given to capital goods purchased from abroad," he argued. And with time, the government would soon impose import licenses to control the diminishing foreign exchange reserves.

* * *

On the question of human resource development, the government policy paper had given a brief indicating that large numbers of high and middle level manpower would be needed to manage various government functions and services. "With such clear evidence of need for skilled manpower," Obama Snr argued, "why would the government sometimes reject scholarships that were offered to Kenyan students by foreign governments?" The government had gotten increasingly pro-British, opposed the student airlifts to the USA and rebuffed moves by other countries of the Eastern bloc to extend aid. "Are we looking a gift horse in the mouth when we refuse scholarships?" He posed. "It should be realised that one person who goes out to study leaves a chance in our universities for another person who would not otherwise have had the chance. This is the reason why we should not be so choosy in what we get in terms of scholarships."

Sooner or later, he warned, the country would regret its decision to turn down the scholarships. By taking the scholarships, Obama Snr thought the country would make greater strides in human capacity development. In subsequent years, the vision of the young Harvard graduate soon became a reality when the Kenyan leadership started relying on foreign manpower to bolster the rapidly expanding Kenyan civil service.

Obama Snr was equally concerned with the chasm between the rich and the poor that seems to be the curse of unmitigated capitalism. In his critique, he expressed his surprise that the paper did not mention the dual characteristic of the economy. "How can we afford to ignore the pockets of this economy which are underdeveloped without some positive statement about their development?" he wondered. In colonial Kenya, the government had only developed the so-called white highlands. Thus the Central Province, some parts of the Rift Valley and some parts of Kericho were well developed while, in the rest of the former 'African reserves', people continued to eke out a living under appalling conditions. He responded:

> *The government talks of dealing only with areas where the returns of any development programme are ostensible. But surely the returns are low only because these areas are and were undeveloped in the beginning. Must we be so short-sighted as to look only into immediate gains when these areas are rotting in poverty? How would these backward areas be monetised and developed unless the government takes a positive stand and does something to correct this lopsided way of development?*

Today, Kenya remains one of the most unequal countries in the world. Writing in the *Sunday Nation*, columnist Murithi Mutiga reflected on Obama Snr's dreams and the inequalities that existed in the country.[3] He reflected on Obama Snr's opposition to the government's 'chlorophyll' model of economic development that meant that all monies would end up in the agriculturally productive 'green' parts of the country, since the prime driver of the economy was agriculture. It was this economic model that sowed the seeds of the vast inequalities in Kenya today. There was no built-in mechanism to compel the government, after receiving tax funds from what were perceived as the productive areas, to redistribute its revenue. The governing elite pumped the money for motorable roads into places such as Central Kenya and Central Rift Valley, arguing that those were the productive zones of the nation.

On 4 August 2010, the dream of Obama Snr was fulfilled when Kenyans repudiated that model by voting overwhelmingly for a constitution that embodied Obama Snr's ideals.

---

[3] Muriithi Mutiga, *Sunday Nation,* 12 September 2010.

The provision in the new constitution that requires the government to redistribute at least 15 per cent of gross national income to the counties is a conscious attempt to tackle inequality. This redirects resources to the grassroots and strips Treasury of its discretionary power to allocate funds as it deems fit.

On the issue of foreign investment, he noted that the government was not committed to any specific and active policy in guiding foreign investors to integrate them within the Kenyan economy. "The government paper had merely outlined how foreign investors could take an active part in the development of the country and sketched areas of social responsibility in which they could take part," Obama Snr contended. "At present, many highly qualified Africans are employed by commercial firms and are given very pompous titles."

However, one would find that they actually have no voice in those companies. "It is strange to note that some of the very big commercial firms deal in some products which are the lifeblood of this country but without the people of this country taking an active part in the formulation of policies thereof," he argued. One may conclude that the absence of a clear policy to integrate the local people into the major investments in the country could have contributed to the massive corruption that is evident in Kenya today.

Striking a rather idealistic vein, the Sessional Paper No. 10 contended that class structures had no place in Africa:

> *The sharp class divisions that once existed in Europe have no place in African Socialism and no parallel in African society. No class problem arose in the traditional African society and none exists today among Africans. The class problem in Africa, therefore, is largely one of prevention, in particular, to eliminate the risk of foreign economic domination; and to plan developments so as to prevent the emergence of antagonistic classes. In addition, Kenya has the special problem of eliminating classes that have arisen largely on the basis of race.*

In regard to the paper's assertion that African society was classless, Obama Snr expressed fears on the growing emergence of a class society in independent Kenya. He talked of the need to eliminate power structures that had been built through excessive accumulation so that not only a few individuals control a vast magnitude of resources as was the case then (and still is). The government needed to adopt a strategy of cure and prevention – not just prevention alone, since a class structure had already emerged in Kenya.

"While we welcome the idea of prevention, we should also try to cure what has seeped in," Obama Snr argued. The elimination of foreign economic and political domination is a good gesture towards this, as are plans to develop in order to prevent antagonistic classes," he argued. "If one says that the African society was classless as the paper says, what is there to stop it from being a class society as time goes on? Is what has been said in the paper, if implemented, enough to eschew this danger?" He clearly thought it was not. "It may be true that African traditions had no parallels in European feudal society so that the problems arising there may not arise here," he added, "but can one be so blind as not to see that all through the colonial period, this same class distinction was transplanted here?"

The Paper also argued that the principle of political equality eliminates the use of economic power as a political base. "It was strange," Obama Snr countered, "that the government could say that yet everywhere – in America, Africa and Europe – the Dollar, the Pound and the Deutsche Mark have been used to devastating effect as political weapons despite professed ideologies." It was alright to be optimistic, he contended, "but so long as private enterprise is given free rein, one would be naive to deny that some would accumulate more than others, nor was it unlikely that in a country with low per capita incomes, to subject the poor into submitting to political ideologies and to persuade them to vote for those who offer them money would be difficult."

* * *

On the sensitive topic of nationalisation, the sessional paper had indicated that nationalisation was a useful tool that had already been used in Kenya and could still be used should circumstances require. The pertinent questions were at what cost, for what purpose, and when. The constitution and the ruling party KANU manifesto made it clear that African Socialism in Kenya did not imply a commitment to indiscriminate nationalisation.

In his response, Obama Snr raised some interesting points. There was likelihood that nationalisation would discourage additional private investment, thus further reducing the rate of growth of the economy, he contended. It was also the case that the use of domestic capital to nationalise would reduce the country's ability to match foreign aid funds, leading to an even greater reduction in development expenditure.

Making reference to Prof Bronferbrenner's work on the *'Appeals for confiscation in Economic Development'*, he broadened the grounds for nationalisation. "Nationalisation should not only be looked at in terms of profitability alone, but also, or even more, on the benefit to the society that such services render and on its importance in terms of public interest," he asserted. If one looked at these things purely on profitability, he continued, the railways would not have been nationalised worldwide since it is the least profitable so that, in all countries, government subsidises it. He also noted that African enterprises did not exist in Kenya and so, if the country was going to nationalise anything, it would only nationalise what existed and what was worth nationalising – the European and Asian enterprises. As he rightly pointed out, most sectors of the economy failed to grow because they remained in state hands.

* * *

The sessional paper also indicated that government's capacity to achieve its desired objectives was restricted by limited resources, and by the high rate of population growth. For Obama Snr, however, population growth *per se* was not the problem. Without proper policies and resource utilisation regimes, there would always be scarcity and low standards of living. He argued thus in his response:

Surely we are not an overpopulated country. We have vast
areas which are lying idle or sparsely populated or which could
be inhabitable if irrigation and proper projects were to be put
under way. We cannot only absorb three times the population
we have now, but even more with proper planning. Further,
we should not only look at the population as consumers of
goods and services, but also as producers of these goods and
services. If we realise this, then we should not be worried about
the rate of growth of population. All we need to think of is to
plan properly and find projects, given priorities, which will
absorb this populace. In this way, we will not only be able to
absorb the rising population growth, but also the overwhelming
disguised unemployment.[4]

Today, a lot of effort is being put to irrigating vast areas of idle land.
These efforts are in sync with Obama Snr's vision.

* * *

On the matter of achieving rapid growth, the sessional paper stated that
the government would borrow from foreign governments and international
institutions and stimulate the inflow of private capital from abroad. The
reason for the low level of domestic capital, countered Obama Snr, was
because the majority of the populace have such a low per capita income
that it is almost impossible for them to save. There was a small minority
of people and worse still, on a racial basis, who had high incomes and
who could afford to rely on one group or a small segment of society
to do all the saving. Sadly, not all of this saving was being invested in
the country. The solution, he suggested, was to redistribute economic
gains to the benefit of all and to channel some of these gains to future
production. "For that reason," he concluded, "the government should
tax the rich more in order to generate high tax surpluses."

The government promised to ensure that, where large amounts of
productive assets must be assembled to achieve economies of scale, the
ownership of these assets would be widely distributed. The methods
to achieve a diffusion of ownership of large-scale enterprises would

---

[4] Barack Obama Snr, *Problems Facing our Socialism,* Available at: *http://www.politico.com/*
static/PPM41_eastafrica.html (Accesed 10 July 2009].

include state ownership, joint ventures by the state with private investors, cooperatives, companies and partnerships.

On the question of land tenure and control of resources, the paper described agriculture as the dominant sector of the economy, encompassing the whole country and providing a living for the majority of its people. Kenya's plans in agriculture provided perhaps the best example of African Socialism at work, the paper said. The progressive Africanisation of ownership would be facilitated through settlement schemes, the paper added. The practice of spending a large proportion of the government budget on the settlement and development of a limited acreage in former European areas should be phased out and future funds channelled to the development of the great potential of the African areas, it added. What was urgently needed was development, not merely land transfer. Consolidation and registration would make farm credit and modern methods of agriculture possible and expand employment much more rapidly than settlement can, by bringing more land into productive use.

In his response, Obama Snr argued that unless productivity is increased, consolidation alone would add relatively little to output, which could only be if the old methods and tools of production are abandoned. "The government will have to play an active part, through the purchase and loaning of more small machinery and intensify the training of people on how to use them in their lands and teaching them intensively ways of rotation of crops, grazing and prevention of erosion," he contended. To this end, he rooted for the creation of more model farms run by the government, which he deemed of greater relevance than the settlement schemes that the government had embarked on immediately after independence.

In response to the paper's contention that traditional African communal ownership models could not be practiced indiscriminately in a modern, monetary economy, Obama Snr commented on the dubious nature of that claim, unless the paper means that what is produced communally cannot be exchanged. "Due to credit requirements," the paper added, "there has to be land titles and registrations." "If this were the case," he responded, "must these land titles and registrations be done only on the basis of individual ownership? Does it mean that cooperatives cannot be registered – or that what is owned in common cannot have title deeds? Is communal ownership of land incompatible with land consolidation?"

"Mismanagement of resources could occur under private as well as public ownership," he reasoned. The country could avoid concentration of economic power and bring about a more standardised use and control of resources through public ownership, let alone the equitable distribution of economic gains that would follow. One need not talk of state ownership of everything from a small garden to a big farm.

Would it not seem, then, that the government could bring more rapid consolidation through clan cooperatives? If the government should feel that individual ownership is the best policy to take in order to bring development, then it should restrict the size of farms that can be owned by one individual throughout the country, and this should apply to everybody – from the president to the ordinary man, he wrote. In the following years, Obama Snr's vision became a reality as the government embraced communal utilities such as group ranches and cooperatives to bolster development. The issue of land ownership became the subject of intense debate in the proposed draft constitution and the referendum on 4 August 2010.

* * *

Obama Snr also had reservations about the skewed nature of the economy as manifested not only in resource ownership, but also in access to the factors of production and investment opportunities. In the Sessional Paper No. 10 of 1965, the government put forward a strong case for Africanisation. It also sought to reconcile the urgency of the matter with citizenship guarantees and the desire for rapid economic growth. To address imbalances in resource ownership between indigenous Kenyans and the Whites and Asians, the most direct way would be to use the government's limited development money to buy existing properties for Africans. Such purchases could be made on a willing buyer-willing seller basis without violating the constitution.

However, such purchases would have the same effect on development as indiscriminate nationalisation; namely, to reduce substantially the amounts the government could spend on development. Further, if such transfers were to be made to untrained, inexperienced people, they would quickly go bankrupt, making Africanisation a temporary rather than a lasting solution. Moreover, as such transfers would reduce the rate of growth, more opportunities for Africanisation might be destroyed than could be created.

In his rejoinder, Obama Snr lamented the overwhelming economic might of the immigrant races over the indigenous Africans. As he rightly noted, the Asians and Europeans owned nearly all commercial enterprises and industries in Nairobi. The African must be economically empowered and given his place in his own country. He exhorted the government to move with speed to redress the imbalances.

"It is laudable that the government came out with the paper," Obama Snr said in his concluding remarks. "But this is not to deny the fact that it could have been a better paper if the government were to look into priorities and see them clearly within their context so that their implementation could have a basis on which to rely."

Obama Senior

In a pensive mood.

In a social mood.

Obama Snr with friends at a party (Amie and Suzie Nachmenoffs house) in Pearl Harbour, Hawaii, 1961.

Obama Snr with Assistant Minister for Tourism J M Kariuki (right) and the PS, Ministry of Tourism (centre).

President Obama with his brother Mark.

Obama Snr at Amie and Suzie Nachmenoffs house in Pearl Harbour, Hawaii, 1961.

Obama Snr (wearing floral loins) on graduation day. Standing next is his father-in-law, Stanley Armour Dunham.

Obama Snr with wife Ruth in Nairobi.

Obama Snr holding his newly-delivered last born son George by Jael, 1982. George was born six months before Obama Snr's death.

Obama Snr's wife Ruth with son Mark.

The young George Obama, 1985.

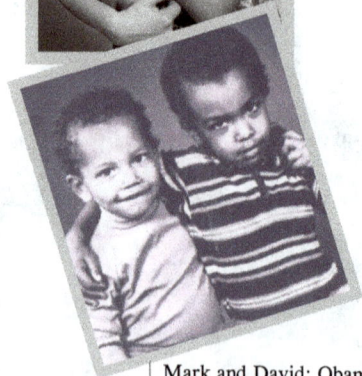

Mark and David: Obama Snr's children by Ruth.

Obama Snr with his wife Ruth and children, Mark and David.

Jael, with their newly-delivered son George, 1982. This photo was taken outside their house in Mawenzi Gardens Estate, Nairobi.

Obama Snr's wife, Jael.

Obama Snr in a pensive mood.

Jael with George (left) and a cousin.

Obama Snr with his children Malik Abong'o (standing extreme right) and Mark Okoth (left) and David (right).

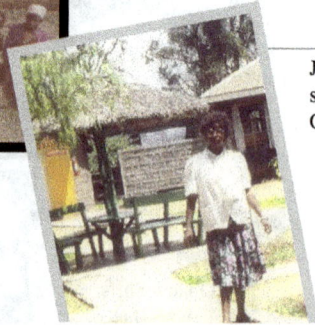

Jael, Obama Snr's fourth wife with friends.

Jael's sister, Janet Onyango.

Habiba Akumu, *nyar* Njoga, Obama Snr's mother sitting next to the coffin of Obama Snr during his burial.

Habiba Akumu, *nyar* Njoga. This photo was taken in her home of the second marriage in K'orele.

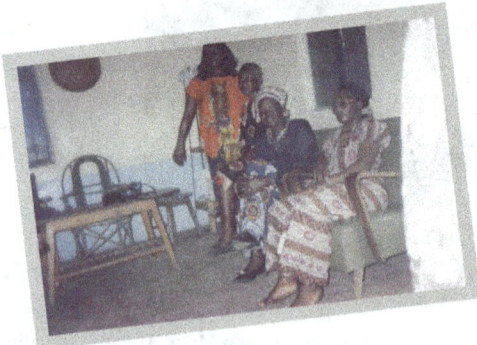

Jael with friends and family members.

Jael with George Obama and a relative.

George Obama with a friend.

George Obama with his French guardian.

George Obama with a friend.

Jael with a friends

Jael with friends.

Ezra with former Minister Shariff Nassir

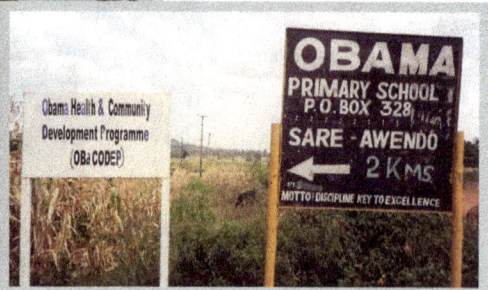

Ezra Obama with his children pose for a photo with his father (in glasses).

Obama Primary School in Migori County, near Obama market next to Obama Health and Community Development Programme. The K'ogelo settled here long ago, hence their influence.

Ezra Obama brother to Obama Snr.

Tom Mboya, the architect of the Kenyan student airlifts to America, 1959-1961.

From left: Ann Dunham, Stanley Dunham, with Maya and Barack Obama.

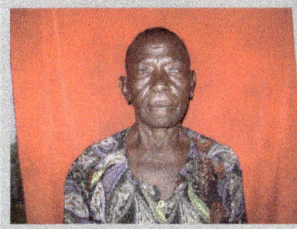
Hawa, Obama Snr's sister.

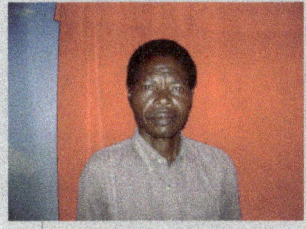
Amir, son of Akumu and brother to Obama Snr.

President Obama with his grandmother during his visit to Kenya when he was Senator.

Ezra Obama with former
Nairobi Mayor Joe Akech.

Obama Snr in
an international
conference

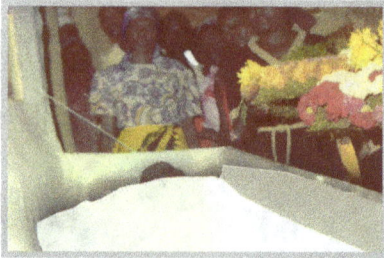

Akumu *nyar* Njoga at
Obama Snr's funeral at
Nyang'oma K'Ogello,
1982.

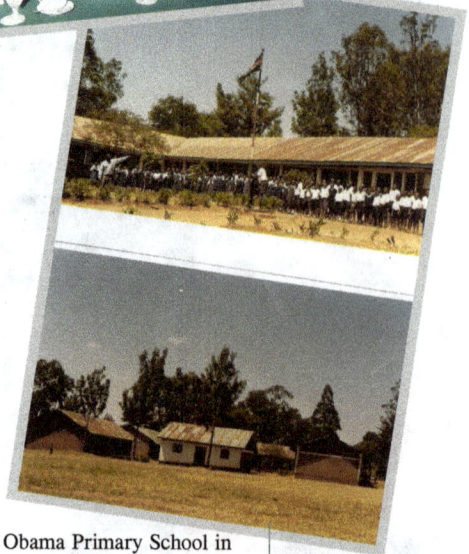

Obama Primary School in
Migori.

David Obama with his uncle at the
funeral of his father, Obama Snr.

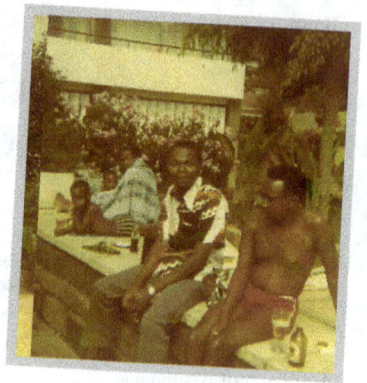

Obama Snr (left) enjoying a drink
with a friend (right) on a swimming
outing with his children.

Chapter 11

Obama Snr the Man: Charm and Charisma

"He was smart, and he couldn't ever let you forget (it). If you came home with the second best grades in class, he would ask why you weren't first.
'You are an Obama,' he would say. 'You should be the best.'"
– Malik Obama

As the University of Hawaii's first African student, Obama Snr could not have stood out more conspicuously. Although Hawaii in the early 1960s offered a somewhat diverse cultural mix, there were notably few African-Americans on the streets of Honolulu. Many people were interested in this high-spirited, opinionated emissary from Africa, and he loved the spotlight. He addressed churches and community groups on race and politics and wrote contributions to newspapers.

His interest in learning and intellectual pursuit predated his sojourn in Hawaii and Harvard in the USA. According to Olara Otunnu, a one time Under-Secretary-General of the UN and Uganda's Minister for Foreign Affairs, Obama Snr was "brilliant, well read, brimming with confidence."[1]

Neil Abercrombie, Democratic Congressman and contemporary of Obama Snr at the University of Hawaii, concurs. "He was a curiosity. He always had an opinion. Anyone can have an opinion, but Barack (Obama Snr) was brilliant and he always had the information to back it up."[2]

---

[1] Tom Shachtman, *Airlift to America*, p. 6.
[2] Sally Jacobs, *"A Father's Charm, Absence"*, *Boston Globe,* 21 September 2008, Available at: http://www.boston.com/news/politics/2008/articles/2008/09/21/a_fathers_charm_absence/ (Accessed 4 January 2014].

Throughout his life, he showed exceptional academic ability. In fact, his rejection of female teachers during his earlier education may have had less to do with sexism and more with astute observation. As a child, he had learnt from his father that male teachers were often more educated than female teachers. The observant lad right away saw that he could get a better education from the male teachers. He willingly paid the price, abandoning the nearby school to trek to Ng'iya School, about seven kilometres away, where he believed he could get a higher quality education.

While at Ng'iya School, he consistently scored the highest marks, recalls Mama Sarah. His father was very strict. This could have contributed to his culture of hard work. His teacher in the new school was a man, but he discovered that it did not solve all his problems. He always knew the answers, and would sometimes even correct the teacher's mistakes before the whole class. The teacher would scold him for his insolence, but he would refuse to back down. That earned him many caning sessions at the hands of the headmaster. But it also taught him something because, the following year, he switched to a class with a woman teacher. "I noticed that he didn't complain (about female teachers any more)," Mama Sarah relates.

Kezia, his *Mikayi* (elder wife) concurs that her late husband was exceptional. "True, he behaved appallingly sometimes," she remarked. "He could be selfish and became disillusioned, but he was also clever and talented," she concluded.[3] Interviewed, Peter Oloo Aringo, a former long-serving Kenyan Minister for Education, and a long-time friend of Obama Snr confirmed that he had gifted brains. "He was bright, smart and intelligent. He was knowledgeable in many fields. He performed extremely well academically and was an intellectual genius," Aringo asserted.

"He was a bright boy," added Dr Francis Masakhalia. "He maintained top grades throughout his studies at Maseno School."

---

[3] John Oywa, Keziah Obama: *My Life with Obama Senior, East African Standard,* 11 November 2008. Available at http://www.standardmedia.co.ke/InsidePage.php?id=1143999026&catid=4 &a=1(Accessed 21 August 2014].

Maseno was then the best school in Western Kenya and among the top four schools in the entire country, the other three being Alliance High School and Mang'u High School both in Central Kenya and Shimo la Tewa at the Coast.

Similar sentiments came from his contemporaries at the University of Hawaii. "He was blessed with razor-sharp intelligence and had made good use of the generous American support," says Neil Abercrombie, who describes him as a straight-A student. The senior Obama was naturally gifted. "While in Harvard, he shared a house with a Nigerian who later became a finance minister in his country. If I remember correctly, his name was Ekukinam," Wasonga added.

While at Harvard, Obama Snr, among other Kenyan students, lived in Boston's 17th Perry Street. During that time, says Wasonga, Obama Snr was involved in endless parties, while his Nigerian housemate covered himself in bed, reading. His Nigerian housemate would complain: "What is wrong with this man? When does he ever read?" He did not have to struggle with his books.

Other comments came from some of his close associates in Nairobi. "I remember him as a brilliant scholar, immensely proud of his academic achievements," says Ogembo. "He fondly talked about his son in the USA, the boy who would one day ascend to the presidency of that great nation. He was an immensely proud and ambitious man who had little respect for non-achievers," recalls Ogembo.

Barack Obama Senior was without doubt one of the inspirations behind President Barack Obama's audacious drive to the most powerful office in the world. True, such a remarkable achievement must be the result of myriad forces of historical proportions, working together in tandem towards an inexorable destiny. Doubtless, many people, places and events contributed in one way or another to inspire President Barack Obama's spirited march to the White House. Still, many analysts would concur that his father, Obama Snr, remains one of the biggest sources of inspiration for the President.

After graduating from the University of Hawaii, Economics Department with top honours, Obama Snr was awarded two scholarships – one to the New School in New York, the other to Harvard. "The New School agreed to pay for everything – room and board, a job on campus, enough to support all three of us," President Barack Obama writes. "Harvard just agreed to pay tuition." Preferring excellence over convenience, he chose Harvard. He had to go to Harvard. "How can I refuse the best education?" he demanded of his wife, Ann. "That's all he could think about, proving that he was the best ..."[4]

Reminiscing about him, one of his sons, Malik Obama, says: "He was smart, and he couldn't ever let you forget (it). If you came home with the second best grades in class, he would ask why you weren't first. 'You are an Obama,' he would say. 'You should be the best.'"[5] No wonder Barack Obama broke all barriers to success.

In 1971, Obama Snr travelled to Hawaii to visit his then ten-year old son. During the month-long visit, he was invited to give a speech at the local Punahou School where the future president was a student. "You have got a pretty impressive father," one of the teachers remarked to the young Barack Obama afterwards. While in Hawaii, father and son attended a concert together and his father gave him a basketball for Christmas. They walked around the city and his father introduced him to old friends from college. They lay side by side on his father's bed reading together.

On the day he left, he gave his son a present – two records of African music that he had brought from Kenya. While father and son would exchange letters through the years, they would never see each other again.[6]

When Ann Dunham visited the adult Barack Obama in Columbia University in 1982, she was particularly pleased to learn that her son planned to visit his father in Kenya. "I think it will be wonderful for you two to finally know each other," she told him.

---

[4] Barack Obama, (2004). *Dreams from My Father*, p. 126.
[5] Barack Obama (2004), *Dreams from My Father*, p. 265.
[6] Steve Dougherty, *Hopes and Dreams*, p. 47.

She shared her memories of Obama Snr, including one story about how he was an hour late for their first date. Waiting for him outside the university library, she had fallen asleep on a bench. She woke up to find her future husband standing over her with two friends. "You see gentlemen," he said, "I told you that she was a fine girl and that she would wait for me." The way she told the story, smiling and laughing as she spoke, gave the younger Barack Obama a glimpse of the depth of her enduring love for his father. "Even though he'd left her with a baby to raise on her own and she had divorced him as a result, she loved him still." As he later wrote, she had tried to make him, "the child who never knew him, see him in the same way."[7]

* * *

Such views were shared by colleagues, friends and family alike. According to Mama Sarah, he was extremely bright, and more exposed than the other sons of Hussein Onyango Obama. "He was a bright man who loved education and development," she says. "For many years, he worked in various positions in the urban centres. He also worked with the white people for many years and was considered one of the lucky few who had been 'urbanised.'"

When a close friend paid him a visit at his house in Woodley Estate in Nairobi, he found the house filled with books on the shelves and on the tables, while others were scattered on the floor. "Why do you keep so many books in your house when you do not read them?" he challenged him. "Are you trying to show off that you are an intellectual when you are not?"

"I don't just keep books. I read them all," Obama Snr responded. And indeed, when he penned his critique of the government's seminal Sessional Paper no. 10 of 1965, he made it clear that matters of education were at the centre of his heart.

But Obama Snr had his weaknesses, too. During his working life, he was embroiled in some rather bizarre incidents. The then General Manager of the Kenya Tourist Development Corporation (KTDC), Jerry Owuor, while confirming in an interview that Obama Snr served

---

[7] Steve Dougherty, *Hopes and Dreams*, p. 47.

in his organisation, added that he thought him a highly self-opinionated individual who lectured instead of contributing to the agenda in meetings. Harvard weighed heavily on his shoulders. He thought he knew everything, while his boss knew next to nothing. His drinking problem resurfaced again to plague him at work, denting his otherwise stellar credentials.

He would often come to work looking a bit dazed, as if he had drank too much the previous evening. Somehow, he still managed to beat his deadlines. In view of his erratic behaviour, the boss felt compelled to supervise him closely. That really incensed him.

His drinking problem caused some scenes that would be hilarious were their consequences on company image not so disastrous. "One Sunday morning, I received a call from Dar es Salaam, Tanzania, where Obama Snr had gone to attend a tourism meeting," Owuor relates. "It was from the Tanzanian Army – asking me if I was the accountant and would I kindly post some bail urgently?" The CEO of KTDC had just been arrested for being drunk and disorderly in the army barracks, the caller explained, and he had instructed that the chief accountant wire money for posting bail. Apparently, Obama Snr kept the charade, telling all and sundry that he was the CEO, which he was not.

"It has been said that the government system was hostile to Obama Snr," Owuor reflects. "My experience is that the few years (that we served together) at KTDC did not corroborate that as I would have noticed it."

Talking of Obama Snr, Ezra says that in his lifetime, his easy self-assurance was often mistaken for vulgar arrogance. "I remember one time at the (Sarova) Panafric Hotel in Nairobi, where we had gone to enjoy some drinks with a friend, Mike Oneko, son of the nationalist Achieng' Oneko," says Ezra. "He soon spotted a lady seated alone at a corner table. "How can a beautiful woman like this sit all by herself?" He jokingly remarked.

"Her boyfriend seemed to have picked up the phrase, and he angrily confronted us. Obama Snr just laughed, and we all joined in good-naturedly and had a hearty laugh. 'The lady is simply ravishing, honestly,' he told him. Mollified, the boyfriend just shook his head and left."

Obama Snr was a deeply honest man, sometimes to the point of embarrassment. He would call a spade a spade and damn the consequences. He could be fearless to the point of being foolhardy.

"I remember an occasion when we had gone for lunch at Kaloleni," adds Ezra. "We found some friends enjoying *nyama choma* (roast meat). Without preamble, he picked one choice piece of morsel that he proceeded to munch appreciatively. The person sitting opposite was incensed.

"How can you pick a piece of meat before you wash your hands?" he demanded furiously.

"Unwashed, my hands are still cleaner than yours even after you have washed them with soap," Obama Snr shot back.

On the whole, says Ezra, he was painfully honest, but generous, sociable and peace loving. It did not really bother him to share anything – whether it was the last coin in his pocket, or a piece of his awesome mind.

During the time when Ezra stayed with the Obamas, their children attended a private nursery and primary school. They later on went to St Mary's School in the Lavington area of Nairobi for their secondary education. Mark Obama was an 'A' student and was the best piano player during all the four years he was at St Mary's School. He is reported to be coaching piano in China and is married to a Chinese lady.

Before proceeding to high school, the other children – Auma and Malik – went to Kilimani Primary School, among others. Abong'o Malik went to Lenana School, then known as Duke of York, while Auma went to Kenya High School, where Ida Odinga, wife of Raila Odinga, Kenya's Prime Minister from 2007-2013, was a teacher. They all did very well in school.

Malik eventually went to the University of Nairobi, while Auma joined Kenyatta University, later on proceeding to Germany for further studies.

Obama Snr was very keen on education, and he encouraged others around him to study. "When I sat for my Kenya Preliminary Education Certificate in 1966, I passed highly, scoring two distinctions and a credit," Ezra recalls. "I was admitted to Maranda Secondary School, but I couldn't make it because of financial difficulties. He invited me to come live with him in his house. He ended up paying up quite a huge part of my school fees."

"I stayed with the Obamas and attended school in Nairobi until I finished high school. The environment in the house was very supportive, as both Obama Snr and Ruth were avid supporters of education. Obama Snr was always at hand to help with the homework and with whatever challenges that arose," says Ezra.

There was no room for idleness or sloth in the Obama household. He would personally inspect the children's school work. Even watching of the television was strictly regulated, being mostly limited to weekends, holidays and special programmes. After dinner at 6 p.m. in the evening, everyone would embark on their homework. The children would take advantage of his absence to watch their favourite programmes on television outside the prescribed hours but switch it off the moment his car hit the driveway.

When the results came through, he would again take time to go through them with the children on the areas of difficulty. "He was always encouraging," says Ezra. "He didn't brook failure or lame excuses, bluntly saying that he expected nothing short of excellent performance. Whatever the grade, he would always encourage the children to perform better."

When parental attention was needed at school, he was quick to respond. He would find time to attend school activities such as open days and parents' days. He wanted the children to be tops. If one was number two, he would ask rhetorically: "But why did you allow somebody else to be number one and you are an Obama? You should be number one and other people can follow you." No wonder his children became exemplary.

The strict discipline extended to other areas, such as the telephone. The house had a telephone connection – a rarity then. Ezra was an eligible young man then, and some calls from the ladies were to be expected. "If a lady friend called me and he happened to be within earshot," Ezra relates, "I would pick up the phone and loudly say, 'Wrong number!' into the mouthpiece. I would see him at the corner of the house, grinning, because he would know I was lying. Afterwards he would say to me,

'Don't lie, that was your call and you pretended that it was not.' He didn't like it so I stopped."

His love of education was all-encompassing; it went beyond the duty of merely educating his children or helping his close relations. "I remember the case of Achieng' Oneko, one of independent Kenya's most prominent politicians who was twice detained –first by the colonial government at the height of the struggle for independence and later by the government of independent Kenya.

"During those days, not many people would be willing to associate with political detainees because of a very real fear of government reprisal. Nevertheless, when Achieng' Oneko's wife asked Obama to help find a school for her children, he helped have them admitted at Kilimani Primary School. That shows how responsible he was in life," Ezra reminisces.

"I remember when I was newly married, and he came to our house with some choice piece of advice," Ezra continues. "The only thing that you can do for your progeny, the only real legacy that you can bequeath your children, is education."

In his social life, Obama Snr was slick and flamboyant. A close friend who regularly socialised with him, Mr Onono, describes him as a social and outgoing character. "He was friendly and charming. He never picked a quarrel with anybody," Onono says. "His main interest was the drinks. You would eat and laugh, dance and laugh, when you were with him. That was the trend." Other friends and contemporaries also remember him as a friendly and fun-loving person.

Flashy and supremely confident, he always had a ready answer. Reverend Nick Ajuoga, a colleague at Shell Oil Company and his neighbour at Woodley Estate also talked about Obama Snr's social life. "Obama Snr belonged to the upper echelons, but he freely conversed with everybody. Most of his senior colleagues at the company were white people and whenever they greeted him, Obama Snr would respond in his distinctive voice, "*Comme ci, comme ça!*" (in French meaning "Not too good, not too bad"). That was his customary way of responding to greetings. In all, he was very cordial and would never pass even a casual acquaintance without a greeting.

In the evenings and on weekends, his haunt of choice was K'Anyim, a popular joint owned by one of his friends in Kaloleni, Nairobi. He also frequented Dala Bar, then a popular joint in the neighbouring Ziwani Estate that has since closed. It was a major meeting place for his kinsmen in Nairobi where he would catch up on social chatter and the events from upcountry while sipping beer and savouring roast meat. Another place that he also frequented was BTM, *Baby Touch Me*, in Athi River on the outskirts of Nairobi where musical entertainment was in plenty and many revellers would dance the night away.

Mama Sarah confirmed that, as a young man, Obama Snr won many dancing competitions. His love of music was part of the rich lore of the Luo. He often took his wife Kezia out for live band performances in far away places such as Kendu Bay.[8]

His prowess on the dance floor is well documented. Perez Ang'awa, a close family friend, remembers him taking to the floor with his wife, Ruth. People would sit back and just watch them, so graceful was their dancing.

He frequented Starlight Club in the centre of Nairobi, which was particularly popular for African jazz music. He was especially taken by the soulful tunes of one musician, Oloo Ranger, who performed regularly at Kaloleni. He greatly loved *nyama choma* (roast meat) and *kuku choma* (roast chicken) as well as *mshikaki* (beef biting) at the present Osewe's of the Ranalo fame. Ranalo Foods is now a major restaurant in Nairobi that is famous for its mouth-watering African dishes.

Obama Snr went further and taught his son how to dance to the African music when he visited him in Hawaii. Obama Snr enjoyed a variety of beats, and was especially attached to Luo traditional music. His love and attachment to music is part of the Luo traditional background. The love of music is deeply rooted in the Luo culture.

At a personal level, Obama Snr was ever cheerful, even in hospital, recalls Rev Nick Ajuoga, who visited him in hospital one time after he

---

[8]   John Oywa, *"Kezia Obama: My Life with Obama Senior," East African Standard,* 11 September 2008.

96

had been involved in an accident. "He had crashed the car against a tree. When we asked him what had happened," Rev Ajuoga explains, "he cheerfully replied: 'I was driving and this tree could just not get off the road, so I had no option but to hit it.'"

A neighbour, Simeon Ochieng, recalls visiting him in hospital to wish him well after an accident. His legs were heavily plastered, but his sense of humour remained irrepressible. And even as Ochieng tried to console him, he boomed back. "This ... this ... this is nothing!" He said, pointing at his legs. "What matters is this," he said, tapping his head amid heavy laughter. Sipping water, he continued, "I can do without them," again pointing at his legs. "As long as I have my brains, which is what matters, I can still perform wonders." Perhaps Obama Snr meant to capture the wisdom behind the Luo saying, *wich e dhano* (brains maketh the human being). While it has been alluded elsewhere that Obama Snr lost both legs in an accident, Mama Sarah vehemently denied that assertion and confirmed that Obama Snr had both his legs intact at the time of his death.

Chapter 12

The Dream Lives On: Like Father, Like Son

"The first time I met President Barack Obama was when he came to Kenya in 1985. He was so much like his father, his looks, his voice – everything. It was like seeing my husband all over again."
– Kezia Obama

The similarities between father and son are striking. They shared the very same names; they both went to Harvard – and later served a short stint as university lecturers. The distinctive deep voice was a shared quality, as was the intellectual prowess and penchant for politics. They both ventured in student politics at an early age: while Obama Snr was expelled from Maseno School for political activism, President Barack Obama participated in a demonstration against apartheid while still in college.[1]

For both of them, their parents separated while they were still young – and subsequently remarried. They both got on well with their new step-parents, and equally maintained good relations with their separated biological parents. Both were big dreamers and would employ their best efforts for the welfare of mankind. Both believed that they were the best: playing second fiddle was not their lot. They were eloquent, confident, diligent, patriotic, generous, extremely social and interactive, and greatly loved their cultures. They both demonstrated great love and affinity to their families. Both were writers – while President Barack Obama has authored two books, Obama Snr is author of a 1959 publication

[1] Barack Obama, *Dreams from My Father*, p. 105.

titled, *Otieno Jarieko* (Otieno the wise man).[2] He also made enormous contributions to the drafting of several policy documents, as well as budget and presidential speeches during his stint at the Ministry of Planning.

Olara Otunnu, a former Ugandan foreign affairs minister and one-time UN Under-Secretary-General, also remarked the great resemblance between father and son. The two, he says, have "the same tall frame and gait" and similar "charisma, supreme confidence and eloquence." Talking about Obama Snr, he remembers his "incredible charismatic presence, very outgoing, charming, talking – (he) would walk into a room and start joking with everyone, a compelling personality."[3] President Obama, he adds, has however "avoided inheriting any of his father's flaws."[4]

Ezra Obama says the similarity between Obama Snr and his son, President Barack Obama, is conspicuous. In the resonance of his deep voice, his gait and the way he moves, the President is almost an exact replica of his father. "In fact," adds Ezra, "Whenever I see him, I often get the strange feeling that I am seeing my old friend and cousin all over again. And when I look at his eyes, and the way he talks, I see the same deep impression of candour that is so easily mistaken for arrogance."

John Oywa who interviewed Obama Snr's first wife, Kezia Obama, in Nairobi after the USA election victory, reported her saying:

> *When I look at my stepson (USA President Barack Obama) he reminds me of his father. They share very many characteristics. Like father, like son, I would say. His father was forthright and loved the truth. This is what I am seeing in his son. The first time I met President Barack Obama was when he came to Kenya in 1985. He was so much like his father – his looks, his voice – everything. It was like seeing my husband all over again.* [5]

[2] Barack Obama (Snr) *Otieno Jarieko,* East African Literature Bureau (Nairobi), 1959.
[3] Tom Schachtman, *Airlift to America,* p. 187 (St Martin's Press, New York, 2009).
[4] Tom Schachtman, *Airlift to America,* p. 236 (St Martin's Press, New York, 2009).
[5] John Oywa, *Kezia Obama: My Life with Obama Senior, East African Standard,* 11 November 2008. Available at: http://www.standardmedia.co.ke/InsidePage. php?id=1143999026&catid=4&a=1 (Accessed 21 August 2014).

The close similarities between father and son befit a saying in the Luo language, *Awendo ki we yieye* (literally, the guinea fowl never changes its spots, but in real sense meaning that the offsprings take after their blood relations).

The first thing that struck people about Obama Snr was his voice. It rose from his depths and rumbled with power. "It was a deep resonant bass with a timbre you could not forget," recalled Richard Hook, who worked with him in the late 1970s as a development adviser for Harvard University's Institute for International Development in Kenya. "He would walk into a room and say, 'My name is Barack Obama, and I am in the Ministry of Finance.' And everyone in the room would instantly look up. Everyone wanted to know who he was."[6]

"Obama Snr had a deep, sonorous voice," adds former Kenya's Minister of Finance, Hon Dr Francis Masakhalia. "While he conversed at his favourite spot at the Nairobi Intercontinental Hotel 'Big Five', you would hear his voice from the hotel's reception desk in the midst of all the noise and bustle of a busy hotel reception and bar."

Neil Abercrombie, a Democratic Congressman from Hawaii compares his voice to American movie star James Earl Jones, who is famous for his deep voice. The Congressman said Obama Snr spoke with a voice so deep that "he made James Earl Jones seem like a tenor."[7]

His voice was unique. "He had a distinctive strong voice so that when he talked behind the walls you would think, 'this must be the chairman of the company'. He also exuded the necessary confidence to go with what he said," narrates Rev Nick Ajuoga. That conspicuous deep voice can also be traced down to his son, USA President Barack Obama. That is the voice that shattered millions of TVs and radios worldwide as President Barack Obama mounted his historic campaigns for the White House.

---

[6] Sally Jacobs, "A Father's Charm, Absence", *Boston Globe,* 21 September 2008. Available at: http://www.boston.com/news/politics/2008/articles/2008/09/21/a_fathers_charm_absence/ (Accessed 4 January 2013].

[7] *Obama's mom Ann Dunham, his dad and grandparents.* Available at: http://blog.edu-cyberpg.com/ 2008/02/12/Obamas+Mom+Stanley+His+Dad+And+Grandparents.aspx (Accessed 24 July 2014)

The voice became one of the most important assets in the presidential drive. It irresistibly conveyed not just hope, but also compassion, authority and power. The voice that had been passed down from father to son became the most powerful voice in the world.

Speaking of how President Barack Obama's voice was central to his success, Shel Leanne describes "his commanding baritone as a natural asset. It sounds pleasing to the ears and is very authoritative." She adds that "effective voice and intonation can move people, make words more memorable, and make the communication more effective overall."[8]

Eloquence is another precious gift that was passed down from father to son. Obama Snr was an accomplished speaker with a good command of English. Both his in-laws acknowledged Obama Snr's eloquence. "He had a voice like black velvet with a British accent and he used it effectively," said Madelyn Dunham, his mother-in-law. Stanley Dunham, his father-in-law, also had a strong message on his eloquence. "He spoke in a deep baritone with a lilting British accent," he said. "He had a strong singing voice full of personality ..."[9] He was also very eloquent.

Sentiments about his eloquence also came from the University of Hawaii. "He had this magnetic personality," remembers Neil Abercrombie, a member of Congress from Hawaii who was friends with him in college. "Everything was oratory from him, even the most commonplace observation." He spoke at church groups and was interviewed for several local newspaper stories. He quickly drew a crowd of friends at the university. "We would drink beer, eat pizza and play records," Abercrombie says. "Everyone had an opinion about everything, and everyone was of the opinion that everyone wanted to hear their opinion – no one more so than Barack (Obama Snr)."[10]

---

[8] Shel Leanne, *Say it like Obama: the Power of Speaking with Purpose and Vision*, p. 26.

[9] Steve Dougherty, *Hopes and Dreams*, p. 43.

[10] Sally Jacobs, *"A Father's Charm, Absence"*, Boston Globe, 21 September 2008. Available at: *http://www.boston.com/news/politics/2008/articles/2008/09/21/a_fathers_charm_absence/* (Accessed 4 January 2014].

Pake Zane, Obama Snr's fellow student at Hawaii, shared a similar opinion. "He spoke with a Kenyan-British accent with a slight touch of Oxford arrogance," he says. "But he was real smart."[11]

This gift of eloquence that had been passed on from father to son would be a crucial asset that put Barack Obama in pole position during the battle for the White House in the November 2008 USA elections.

Public speaking is no doubt one of the most important elements in politics. If the message does not get out, then innovative ideas, creative talents and heartfelt beliefs will have no effect. Eloquence can make all the difference. And it made the difference for Barack Obama. During the election campaign, there was attestation from friends and foes alike that Barack Obama's eloquence was beyond reach.

Like his father, Barack Obama displayed impressive oratorical skills. "The words often invoked to describe Barack Obama – magnetic, electrifying, energising and inspiring – speak of his charisma as a leader."[12]

Confidence is another important element that was unique in Obama Snr. In his book, *Dreams from My Father*, President Barack Obama acknowledges learning from his father that confidence is the secret to a man's success.[13]

Obama Snr was renowned for his confidence. He was bold and articulate in speaking out his mind even on sensitive issues, without fear of victimisation. Such bravery was unheard of in African countries, where the rule of law was at best tenuous and rule by fiat the norm. Such candour naturally put him on a collision course with his colleagues and superiors at work – and with the powers that be.

He had no fear, Olara Otunnu remembers. If Obama Snr appeared to some as arrogant, Otunnu views his attitude differently. "He would listen carefully to your argument, and then tear into you with facts and figures. He could be very forthright and that could be annoying to some people."[14]

---

[11] David Remnick, *The Bridge*, p. 52.

[12] Shel Leanne, *Say it Like Obama: The Power of Speaking with Purpose and Vision*, p. 22.

[13] Barack Obama (2004). *Dreams from My Father*, p. 8.

[14] Tom Schachtman, *Airlift to America*, p. 191 (St Martin's Press, New York, 2009).

Francis Mayaka, a former colleague at the Ministry of Planning, says that Obama Snr carried his characteristics even to the boardroom. He would take anybody to task – his bosses, donors and international guests alike – if he felt that their contributions were not up to standard. And he expressed such sentiments with confidence that left everyone perplexed.

His old colleague in Hawaii, Neil Abercrombie, described him as a man with:

> '... *a big smile, easy to meet, incredibly smart, and he was exotic in the land of the exotic. He was somebody new. In this world of the incredible spectrum of color and eye shapes and physiognomy, he stood out from even that mélange and he had this electric vitality. There was this absolutely dynamic aura about him.* '[15]

Obama Snr was not directly involved in politics, like his son President Obama; however, politics ran deep in his blood. He never entered mainstream politics, but his character, sentiments, attributes and actions were in every respect political. As a student in Maseno School, he ventured into student politics early in life and was expelled by the school authorities in circumstances that had strong political connotations.

"As a young political activist, Obama Snr came to the end of his life prematurely," remembers Kenya's former Minister for Finance, Hon Dr Francis Masakhalia, a schoolmate and long-time colleague of Obama Snr.

"He had not ventured into competitive politics, but was, nevertheless, intensely political. Before he went abroad for university studies, Obama Snr served for some months in 1958 as an executive officer of the Nairobi People's Convention Party (NPCP) led by Tom Mboya. It took a lot of courage during that colonial period for a young man to serve in such a political position. The emergency was still in force. Politicians and their associates were harassed a lot."

During the colonial period, and especially during the struggle for independence, many Kenyans of all shades bore the brunt of repression.

---

[15] David Remnick, *The Bridge*, p. 51.

Obama Snr did not escape the repercussions of the freedom struggle. He, too, was detained by the colonial authorities owing to his political activities and close association with freedom leaders such as Tom Mboya.

In the year 1958, Obama Snr was one of the prospective students who got an opportunity to study in the United States. Before their departure, all students who were to travel were taken through pre-airlift classes meant to introduce them to America and counsel them on how to make it as students in a foreign country. However, immediately they arrived in New York, some students participated in a demonstration demanding for independence. "We want *uhuru* (freedom) now!" "Release Kenyatta now!"[16] They shouted at the arrivals lounge of the New York airport. Independence for Kenya was still several years away and founding president Jomo Kenyatta was still in detention. The students had pushed Kenyan politics to the global arena and more was still to come.

While he was a student at the University of Hawaii in the United States, Obama Snr played a prominent role in student politics. He helped organise the International Students Association, of which he became the first president. His friends were legion and he would team up with them and talk about culture, poetry and music. But politics ran deeply in his blood and he would steer the topic to politics, particularly the anti-colonial wave in Africa.

For one to rise from perceived obscurity to the pinnacle of power, one needs to be fit for the challenge. Without doubt, many factors contributed to Barack Obama's victory among them the strong personality and intelligence that he got from his father.

---

[16] Kamau Ngotho, "Granny of the airlifts", *East African Standard* (Accessed 10 June 2014).

POSTSCRIPTS

Postscript 1: The Race to the White House

"We hold these truths to be self-evident; that all men are created equal, that they are endowed by their Creator with certain inalienable rights; that among these are Life, Liberty and the pursuit of Happiness."
– American Declaration of Independence

On 20 January 2009, Barack Hussein Obama made history as the first African-American president of the United States of America since its founding in 1776. Congratulatory messages poured in from across the globe with Kenya proclaiming a national holiday. For the first time, the world appeared to be speaking with one voice in giving a standing ovation for the new US President.

A pointer to what the world thought of the watershed event and its portent may be gleaned from the reactions and messages that poured in from all corners of the globe. For one, his election proved that America remains the land of the possible, that the American dream lives on, and that the power of American democracy is real. Shortly after his victory, the President set the tone in his speech: "The true strength of our nation comes not from the might of our arms or the scale of our wealth, but from the enduring power of our ideals: democracy, liberty, opportunity and unyielding hope."

Around the world, people celebrated his election as if he were their own and held exceedingly high expectations for his presidency. Spontaneous celebrations erupted in Europe, Asia and Africa, including in Indonesia, where Barack Obama lived as a child, and Kenya, home to the Obama patriarchs. Jubilation swept the Caribbean, which viewed the election of a black president as historic. The healing power of President Barack Obama's victory also resonated in the larger world where leaders from all corners of the earth extended hands of fellowship to the new president. Many world leaders hailed Americans for giving humanity reason to celebrate by rewriting their history and that of the world and redefining crucial global issues such as colour and race.

Sentiments came from as far as China and beyond. Chinese President Hu Jintao said in a statement that he looked forward to working with President Obama to "continuously strengthen dialogue and exchanges between our two countries and enhance our mutual trust and cooperation." Pakistan's Prime Minister, Yousaf Raza Gilani said the election "marks a new chapter in the remarkable history of the United States."

The victory was also greeted with cheers in Mexico, where former foreign minister Jorge Castaneda wrote in the *Reform* newspaper that the presidency represents a chance for Mexico to remake its relationship with the United States. In his message of congratulations, the late President Umar Yar'Adua of Nigeria described Barack Obama's victory as the tearing down of the "greatest barrier of prejudice in human history" as well as a "defining moment in the evolutionary history of the democratic world."

And, from Germany where he had addressed a mammoth crowd during his tour of Europe at the height of the campaigns, Chancellor Angela Merkel said: "The world faces significant challenges at the start of your term. I am convinced that Europe and the United States will work closely and in a spirit of mutual trust together to confront new dangers and risks and will seize the opportunities presented by our global world." Indian Prime Minister Manmohan Singh said Barack Obama's "extraordinary journey to the White House will inspire people not only in the United States but also around the world." French President Nicolas Sarkozy said: "With the world in turmoil and doubt, the American people, faithful to the values that have always defined America's identity, have expressed with force their faith in progress and the future."

There were also messages from both Kenya and Indonesia, the countries where Obama has family links. From Indonesia, President Susilo Bambang Yudhoyono said: "Indonesia especially hopes that the US, under new leadership, will stand in front and take real action to overcome the global financial crisis, especially since the crisis was triggered by the financial conditions in the US." From Kenya, President Mwai Kibaki sent his massage: "We, the Kenyan people are immensely proud of your Kenyan roots. Your victory is not only an inspiration to millions of people all over the world, but it has special resonance with us here in Kenya."

President Dmitry Medvedev of Russia also sent his message. "We hope that our partners – the new US administration – will make a choice in favour of full-fledged relations with Russia." The Israeli Foreign Minister Tzipi Livni called it "a mark of merit for American democracy."

However, the intractable challenge of the Middle East attracted different opinions. Some Arabs and Jews in the Middle East were sceptical that President Barack Obama would bring about real change in the troubled region. "It's the same politics," said a young man from an Israeli-Arab village, "He may change some things in America, maybe in Iraq, but the Palestinian case is really hard to solve. It's complicated." On the other hand hawkish Israelis feared Obama would be more sympathetic to Palestinians and push for the division of Jerusalem in a peace deal. Indeed, Israel was one of the few countries that preferred Republican John McCain in pre-election opinion polls.

* * *

Prior to February 2004, President Barack Obama was relatively unknown in national politics. His first opportunity to make a national impact came when he was invited to deliver the keynote speech at the Democratic National Convention in Boston, Massachusetts in July 2004. That speech marked a turning point in his political career. He utilised the opportunity to speak about changing the US government's economic and social priorities, while questioning the Bush administration's management of the Iraq War and obligations to American soldiers. He criticised heavily partisan views of the electorate and asked Americans to find unity.

"Let's face it," he proclaimed in that historic speech that propelled him to fame, "my presence on this stage is pretty unlikely. My father was a foreign student, born and raised in a small village in Kenya.

He grew up herding goats, went to school in a tin-roof shack. My grandfather was a cook, a domestic servant to the British."

In the speech witnessed by 9.1 million viewers, he explained how his grandfather had larger dreams for his son and how, through hard work and perseverance, his father got a scholarship to study in America – the land of hope and opportunity. While studying, his father met his mother who was born in a town on the other side of the world – Kansas. His parents shared not only an improbable love, but also an abiding faith in the possibilities of the American nation. His parents gave him an African name, Barack, or 'blessed,' believing that in a tolerant America a name is no barrier to success. As he added, his parents imagined him going to the best schools in the land, even though they weren't rich, "… because in a generous America one doesn't have to be rich to achieve his potential."

Barack Obama first entered mainstream politics when he was elected to the Illinois Senate in 1996. He was re-elected to the Illinois Senate in 1998, and again in 2002. Earlier in 2000, he had lost a Democratic primary run for the US House of Representatives to four-term incumbent Bobby Rush by a margin of two to one. This loss turned out to be a blessing because he was then free to run for the US Senate in the subsequent years, a move which would open for him the doors to the White House.

In mid-2002, he began considering a run for the US Senate. He formally announced his candidacy in January 2003. There was initially a wide-open Democratic and Republican primary contest involving fifteen candidates. As he later wrote, "It was a difficult race and crowded field of well-funded, skilled and prominent candidates." Without organisational backing or personal wealth, and being black and saddled with what was perceived as a funny name, he was considered a long shot. In a victory that signaled broader change in racial politics, he won an unexpected landslide victory with 53% of the vote in a seven-candidate field, 29% ahead of his nearest Democratic rival.

In the November 2004 general elections, he received 70% of the vote to Keyes' 27%, the largest victory margin for a statewide race in Illinois history. Following his election to the US Senate in November 2004, he resigned from the Illinois Senate. He was sworn in on January 4, 2005, becoming the fifth African-American Senator in US history and the third to have been popularly elected. He became the only Senate member of the Congressional Black Caucus. In December 2006, President George Bush signed into law the *Democratic Republic of Congo Relief, Security, and Democracy Promotion Act*, marking the first federal legislation to be enacted with Barack Obama as its primary sponsor.

Senator Barack Obama held assignments on the Senate Committees for Foreign Relations, Environment and Public Works, and Veteran's Affairs through December 2006. He made official trips to Eastern Europe, the Middle East, Central Asia and Africa. He met with Mahmoud Abbas before he became president of the Palestinian Authority.

During his trip to Africa, he visited five countries, Ethiopia, Chad, Djibouti, South Africa and Kenya. It was during that trip to Africa, especially in his father's homeland of Kenya, that both Barack Obama and Michelle first got a sense of destiny. The people received him as celebrity and the crowds sang for him. Liza Mundy recounts the experience thus:

On this trip, the worship of Obama reached new heights. Citizens lined streets, perched on balconies, sat on outcroppings of building facades, eager and ultimately ecstatic to see a son of Kenya who had risen so far so fast, in the most powerful nation on earth.

Adults and children alike chanted his name, and often sang it – Obamaobamaobamaobama – until it ceased being a name and became an ululation. There was drumming and dancing everywhere. "It was completely overwhelming, it's hard to describe unless you were there …"[1]

Since the famous Democratic Convention speech in 2004, he had regularly received requests to run for president, but he apparently had not given the idea much thought. At one moment, his daughter Malia asked him, "Are you going to run for president?" Liza Mundi writes:

It was the question on everybody's mind. People had started asking him that question the day after the keynote. After Obama won the Senate election, the question would be incessant, almost obligatory. Diane Sawyer asked. Tim Russert asked. Wolf Blitzer asked. The answer was always: Obama would serve out his six-year Senate term.[2]

[1] Liza Mundi, *Michelle: A Biography*, pp. 264-265.
[2] Op. cit. p. 250.

After that Kenya trip in late 2006, however, everything changed. When Tim Russert asked Barack Obama again whether he would run for president in 2008, he acknowledged, "I have thought about it."[3] According to David Axelrod, the crowds in Kenya "gave him a heightened sense of what he could accomplish."[4]

Finally, the big day came. On 10 February 2007, Barack Obama announced his candidacy for President of the United States in front of the Old State Capitol building in Springfield, Illinois. This was the site where Abraham Lincoln delivered his historic "House Divided" speech in 1858.

The formal entry to the race framed a challenge that was daunting even to the most talented politician: whether Barack Obama, with all his strengths and limitations, could win in a field dominated by Senator Hillary Rodham Clinton, who had years of experience in presidential politics, a command of policy and political history, and an extraordinarily battle-tested network of fund-raisers and advisers. He viewed Hillary Clinton as his biggest challenge, though his aides remained wary as well of former Senator John Edwards, another rival for the Democratic nomination. He also faced a serious onslaught from opposing groups, some of who dubbed him a terrorist. Nevertheless, he soldiered on. He well knew the meaning of the saying: "If you chase every dog that barks, you will never reach your destination."

During the campaigns, Barack Obama drew strength from his previous work, which had taken him to some of Chicago's poorest neighbourhoods, where he had joined with pastors and lay people to deal with communities that had been ravaged by plant closings. He saw that the problems people faced weren't simply local in nature – that the decision to close a steel mill was made by distant executives. He also noted that the lack of textbooks and computers in schools could be traced to the skewed priorities of politicians a thousand miles away; and that when a child turns to violence, there's a hole in his heart no government could ever fill. As he later remarked, it was in these neighbourhoods that he received the best education he ever had.

---

[3] Op. cit., p. 266.
[4] Op. cit., pp. 266-267.

After three years, he went to law school for, as he said, he wanted to understand how the law should work for those in need. He became a civil rights lawyer and taught constitutional law. He came to understand that the cherished rights of liberty and equality depend on the active participation of an awakened electorate. It was with these ideas in mind that he arrived in Illinois as a state Senator. It was in Springfield where he saw all that is America converge – farmers and teachers, businessmen and labourers, all of them with a story to tell, all of them seeking a seat at the table, all of them clamouring to be heard. It was in that period that, as he said, he learned to disagree without being disagreeable, knew it was possible to compromise so long as one knows those principles that can never be compromised; and that so long as there was a will to listen to each other, one can assume the best in people instead of the worst.

Initially, a large number of candidates entered the Democratic Party presidential primaries. After the early contests, the field narrowed to a contest between Barack Obama and Senator Hillary Clinton, with the race remaining close throughout the primaries. On 31 May, the Democratic National Committee agreed to seat all the disputed Michigan and Florida delegates at the national convention, each with a half a vote, narrowing Barack Obama's delegate lead. During the campaign, the often negative contest between Barack Obama and Hillary Clinton dominated the media as well as public attention. Republican candidate John McCain received far less attention from the media or the public.

Barack Obama ran a memorable campaign that sought to provide answers to America's problems at a time when a worsening financial crisis and an impending recession threatened the very essence of the American dream. He seized every opportunity to answer Americans' questions on the policy direction of his government. His steady stream of super delegate endorsements, combined with the delegates he received from the primaries, put him past the 2,118 threshold. On June 3, with all states counted, Barack Obama was named the presumptive Democratic nominee.

In what he called a "defining moment," he became the first African-American ever to head the ticket of a major US political party. "Tonight we mark the end of one historic journey with the beginning of another – a journey that will bring a new and better day to America," he declared after the victory. "Tonight, I can stand before you and say that I will be the Democratic nominee for president of the United States."

He eventually delivered his acceptance speech titled, "The American Promise" during the Democratic National Convention on August 28, 2008 in Denver, Colorado. The speech was viewed by over 38 million people worldwide. Again, he reminded the audience of the speech he had made four years earlier – of the brief union between a young man from Kenya and a young woman from Kansas who were not well off or well known, but shared a belief that in America, their son could achieve whatever he put his mind to.

During both the primary process and the general election, Barack Obama's campaign set numerous fundraising records, particularly in the quantity of small donations. On 9 June 2008, he became the first major-party presidential candidate to turn down public financing in the general election since the system was created in 1976.

In November, Barack Obama won the US presidency with 52.9% of the popular vote to John McCain's 45.7% and 365 electoral votes to 173 to become the first African-American President of the USA. In a victory speech delivered before thousands of supporters in Chicago's Grant Park, President-elect Barack Obama proclaimed the new reality: "Change has come to America."

* * *

President Barack Obama enjoyed many achievements during his two terms in office. In foreign policy, these include the conclusion of a tentative nuclear deal with Iran, which was announced on 2 April, 2015. The deal was reached after negotiations in the framework of the P5+1 group that include Britain, Germany, France, Russia and China. The deal aims to prevent Iran's development of nuclear weapons in return for easing of sanctions in place since 2005. Also, in December 2014, President Barack Obama announced a change in USA policy towards Cuba after

53 years of trade sanctions and travel restriction that were imposed in 1962 following the communist takeover of the Caribbean island in 1959. On 11 April 2015, he became the first US President to meet a Cuban President since 1959, when he met with President Raul Castro in Panama. Soon thereafter, he removed Cuba from the list of nations that sponsor terrorism, where it had been since 1982.

On 21 May 2011, President Obama announced that all USA combat troops would be out of Iraq by end of 2011. This move would end eight years of US combat presence in Iraq that cost over 4,000 American lives. In May 2014, President Obama also announced that he would reduce the number of US troops in Afghanistan to only 10,000 by end of 2014. Specifically, he would reduce the troops in non-combat roles gradually until 2016 when a total withdrawal is expected. This was America's longest war, lasting 12 years and costing 2,312 American lives. Thus, he has fulfilled his election promise to end USA's involvement in the two wars.

On the domestic front, President Obama took action to fix the US immigration system. Under the executive orders issued on 21 November 2014, parents of US citizens and lawful permanent residents would be allowed to apply for deportation deferrals and work permits, a move that was expected to prevent the deportation of 3.7 million adults. Also, on 23 March, 2010, the President signed into law the Patient Protection and Affordable Care Act (ACA), representing the most significant regulatory overhaul of the USA healthcare system since the passage of Medicare and Medicaid in 1965. The ACA was enacted to increase the quality and affordability of health insurance, lower the uninsured rate by expanding public and private insurance coverage, and reduce the costs of healthcare for individuals and the government.

Postscript 2: The Obama Heritage

The Republic of Kenya is located in East Africa. To the north, it is bordered by Ethiopia, renowned for its world conquering long distance athletes, unsettled Somalia to the east, stable Tanzania to the south, fertile Uganda to the west, and strife-torn South Sudan to the northwest, with the Indian Ocean running along the southeast border. Before 1920, the area now known as Kenya was called the British East Africa Protectorate. From east to west, the equator bisects it right through the middle. The Great Rift Valley dissects the country from north to south on its way from Jordan to Mozambique. In the far west is Lake Victoria, Africa's largest lake and one of the sources of the River Nile – and adjacent to Obama Snr's birthplace at Ka'Nyadhiang in Kendu Bay. The lake is shared with Uganda and Tanzania.

The country's physical features provide a veritable paradise for the nature lover. Its world-famous highland region, which lies both east and west of the Rift Valley, is generally cool with a lot of good agricultural land. The Great Rift Valley is unique with its beautiful landscapes and variety of lakes, flora and fauna. Travelling across the country, one would scarcely fail to notice the Nyika plateau, which is a dry, lowland region that is mainly suitable for ranching and pastoral activities. The Great Rift Valley is also home to unique and world-famous animal sanctuaries, such as the Masai Mara game reserve, which is home to world-class tourist hotels and lodges. It is here that you can experience "One of the greatest spectacles on earth" – the great annual wildebeest migration that has now been designated the "Eighth New Wonder of the World". If you follow the Sun's journey across the country, you eventually arrive at the verdant and culturally rich Lake Victoria Basin – home to Obama Snr's people, the Luo.

A visit to Kenya would be incomplete without experiencing first-hand the delights of the Kenyan coast. The coast boasts of roughly 400 km of pristine beaches and palm trees. It is also home to several historical monuments such as Fort Jesus, built by early Portuguese explorers, and the UNESCO World Heritage Site in Lamu. The port of Mombasa is an important gateway serving several countries in the region. Peter Borchert, founder of Africa Geographic magazine, puts it more bluntly: "If you go to just one destination in Africa, let it be Kenya, where the experience we know as the 'Safari' was invented."

Kenya is a country rich in cultural diversity. It is made up of about 42 different ethnic identities, some of which could be seen as separate nationalities forced together by historical circumstances. The five major tribes in Kenya are Kikuyu, Luhya, Kalenjin, Luo and Kamba which together account for about 70% of the total population. The 42 ethnic groups are broadly divided into three main groups – the Bantu, Nilotes and Cushites. Andrew Fedders and Cynthia Salvadon have ably captured the story of the people and cultures of Kenya.[1] In another book, *Kenya's Ethnic Communities: Foundation for a Nation,* Wanguhu Ng'ang'a also gives details of the ethnic groups in Kenya.

The Luo, from whom Obama Snr hails, has a rich history. Before migrating to Kenya and other neighbouring countries, majority of the Luo-speaking people occupied the region south of the confluence of the Nile and the Bahr el Ghazal in South Sudan. In the present day, the Luo-speaking people are to be found mainly along the River Nile and its sources in six countries in the Eastern Africa region that includes Rwanda, South Sudan, Ethiopia, Democratic Republic of Congo, Uganda, Kenya and Tanzania. The Shilluk, who are known by their local name of Dhok Chollo, are the most prominent Luo-speaking ethnic group in South Sudan. Out of about 60 ethnic groups in South Sudan, the Luo speaking Shilluk are the third largest ethnic group after the Dinka and Nuer.[2] Other Luo-speaking groups in South Sudan are Acholi, Pari, Thur, Anyuak or Anywaa, Jurchol, Bor, Brun, Funj, Jo-Luo of Bhar el Ghazal, Maban and Jumjum. Luo speaking peoples in Uganda include the Acholi, Lang'o, Labwor, Jonam, Palwo, Alur, Padhola and Kumam.

---

[1] Andrew Fedders and Cynthia Salvadon, *Peoples and Cultures of Kenya,* TransAfrica\Rex Collings, Nairobi, 1979.

[2] http://www.joshuaproject.net/countries.php?rog3=SU

In Ethiopia, the Luo-speaking people are the Anyuak. Others are the Alur in the Democratic Republic of Congo and the Jo-Luo both in Kenya and Tanzania. There are different Luo dialects spoken in the six countries occupied by the Luo people. The differences can easily be noticed in the various Luo-English dictionaries in circulation in the region.

Due to their unique occupation of the River Nile valley, the Luo are also referred to as River-Lake Nilotes or Western Nilotes. The word 'Nilote' means 'of the Nile' or 'belonging to the Nile'. There is a general belief that the name 'Luo' is derived from the Luo word, *Luwo,* which means "to follow". Thus the language derives its name from the movement of the Luo people along the Nile.[3] Quite apart from deriving their identity from the Nile, the river itself may have borrowed its very name from the Luo. The word 'Nile' in the Luo-Alur dialect means 'big', 'wide', 'long', 'massive', 'endless' – a typical description of the Nile, which is the longest river in the world.

* * *

In the present day, African Kingdoms of Luo origin continue to thrive in Eastern Africa and the Great Lakes region. Even though their power and influence has greatly been reduced, they endure in their great symbolism and as centres of cultural identity. The present-day Luo people still uphold monarchies with strong historical links to the Egyptian Kingdoms. In a major contrast to both Islamic and Christian funerals, they still observe elaborate funeral rites. They also hold to a strong belief in the afterlife.

In his French publication, *Introduction a l'etude des institutions sociopoliques du peuple Alur* ("Introduction to the study of sociopolitical institutions of the Alur people"), a notable intellectual and Member of Parliament in the Democratic Republic of the Congo, Gilbert Umvor Keno *Wod'Ukumu,* (son of Ukumu) has written one of the most instructive pieces available on traditional kingship practices of the Alur people.[4]

---

[3] Peter Firstbrook, *The Obamas*, p. 31.
[4] Gilbert Umvor Keno Wod' Ukumu, *Introduction a l'etude des institutions sociopoliques du peuple Alur* (Introduction to the study of socio-political institutions of the Alur people], Unpublished thesis, Bunia, 2007.

A popular proverb that is still extant among the Luo-speaking Alur people is: *"Wiyi tek chal kana pa Farao"* ('you are as stubborn as Pharaoh's horses.')

What is not in doubt is the fact that, for a long time, ancient Egypt was ruled by African dynasties that have collectively been referred to as the Black Pharaohs. The black pharaohs sprang from a robust African civilisation that had flourished on the southern banks of the Nile for 2,500 years, going back at least as far as the first Egyptian dynasty.

Today, Sudan's more than 200 pyramids – greater in number than all of Egypt's – are haunting spectacles in the Nubian Desert. Strangely, while thousands of tourists flock to the Egyptian pyramids each day, the Sudanese pyramids remain obscure.[5] The entire Nile valley occupied by the Luo and other African peoples may yet prove to be the unexplored "Valley of the Kings."

A notable black ruler, King Piye, ruled over his own kingdom in the present-day Sudan. In the year 730 BC, he invaded and conquered Egypt – and thus initiated a dynasty of the so-called black pharaohs – who ruled over all of Egypt for three-quarters of a century as that country's 25th dynasty. The black pharaohs reunified the tattered country and filled its landscape with glorious monuments, creating an empire that stretched from the southern border at present-day Khartoum all the way north to the Mediterranean Sea.[6] In modern times, Sudan has emerged as one of the most significant archaeological regions in the world. What's more, the earliest Sudanese civilisation is one of the most ancient African cultures. It flourished as a totally independent political entity for at least 15 centuries – until around 1500 BC.[7]

---

[5] Robert Draper, *Black Pharaohs, An ignored chapter of history tells of a time when kings from deep in Africa conquered ancient Egypt,National Geographic. Available at:* ngm. nationalgeographic.com/2008/.../robert-draper-text.html (Accessed 20 July 2014].

[6] Robert Draper, *Black Pharaohs, An ignored chapter of history tells of a time when kings from deep in Africa conquered ancient Egypt, National Geographic. Available at* http://ngm.nationalgeographic.com/print/2008/02/black-pharaohs/robert-draper-text (Accessed 20 December 2014]

[7] Claude Rilly, Kush: *Black Africa's earliest civilisation,* Available at http://www.culturekiosque.com/aboutus/contactus.html (Accessed 3 September 2014]

The link between the Luo people and the pharaohs has been widely studied by reputable researchers and writers – among them Henri Frankfort, C A Diop, Dr Terence Okello Paito, Simon Simonse, JB Webster and Crazzolara, among others. To start with, Henri Frankfort, an eminent Egyptologist, suggested that there are distinct groups of Africans surviving today whose ancestors can be traced back to the ancient Egyptians. Diop in particular, resolved to carry out a comparison of the languages of ancient Egypt and those of contemporary Africa.[8]

In his work, *The African Origin of Civilisation*, Cheikh Anta Diop adopts a multi-faceted approach that reflects his varied background as "historian, physicist, and philosopher". Indeed, he has been singled out as "the only Black African of his generation to have received training as an Egyptologist". He also had direct contact with the oral traditions and social structure of West Africa. "We have come to discover that the ancient Pharaonic Egyptian civilisation was undoubtedly a Negro civilisation. To defend this thesis, anthropological, ethnological, linguistic, historical and cultural arguments have been provided ...,"[9] he told the First International Congress of Black Writers and artists in September 1956.The Cheikh Anta Diop University, also known as the University of Dakar and which has an enrollment of over 60,000, is named after him.

Joy Adamson is known to millions by her books describing the story of Elsa, the celebrity Kenyan lioness. During her life and extensive travels in Kenya over the period prior to independence, she documented many African peoples and cultures.

In one of her encounters with the Luo people, she met a son of the legendary Luo hero, Okore Ogonda, at Nyahera in Kisumu. In her book, *The Peoples of Kenya*, she later wrote:

> *I was struck by the resemblance between his ornaments and*
> *the basic design of the royal insignia of a pharaoh, only that*

---

[8] Cheikh Anta Diop, *The African Origin of Civilisation: Myth or Reality?* New York, L. Hill, 1974.

[9] Cheik Anta Diop, *The African origin of civilisation: Myth or reality, passim.*

118

these were made of local material. The regal wig of a pharaoh was replaced by a broad and beautifully carved ivory frame; the regal beard had become a solid ivory tusk. Instead of the golden chain of Egyptian kings, he wore strings of python vertebrae, but the brass earrings were almost identical with the Egyptian designs and so were the bluish-green beads. "[10]

She was also struck by the regal head dress of a Luo woman that she encountered. It reminded her of "Queen Nefertiti, with the difference that hers was made of beads." In all, Adamson said the ornaments of the two models recalled emblems of one of the most highly developed cultures – ancient Egypt.[11]

---

[10] Joy Adamson, *The Peoples of Kenya*, pp 156–157
[11] Joy Adamson, The Peoples of Kenya, loc cit.

Appendices

2 July 1997

C.B. Sanyo
The Department of the Administrator-General
Public Trustee
P.O. Box 62492
Nairobi, Kenya

Re: Hussein Obama - Deceased
Admin. Cause No. 310 of 1983
Succ. Cause No. 63 of 1990

Dear Mr. Sanyo:

Please be informed that as one of the children of the above referenced deceased, Hussein Obama, I hereby forego any and all claims that I might otherwise have on the deceased's estate, whatever the nature of that estate might be. Please feel free to contact me at the following address if you require any further information on this matter:

Barack Hussein Obama II
5450-1 S. East View Park
Chicago, Illinois 60615
United States of America

Thank you for your assistance.

Sincerely,

Barack Hussein Obama, II

cc: Abongo Malik Obama
Michael Ownor, Esq.

REPUBLIC OF KENYA

MR. MARK NDESANDJO
10 COURTRIGHT ROAD
NEW JERSEY, U.S.A.
(201) 702 7835.

ADMIN. CAUSE NO. 310 OF 1983

I am currently handling this file, and have just stumbled on your letter
to us and attentioned to one Mr. Obama and a Mr. Sanyo dated the 7/30/1997.

It appears from the record that no reply was given to the letter and
the queries you had posed.

I wish to answer your questions as truthfully as I can, that your father
died on the 26th November, 1982 through a road accident.

That grant of letters of administration were issued jointly to one
Malik Abongo Obama, a son of the deceased, and Mrs. Jael Atieno Obama,
the widow of the deceased.

The Ministry of Finance and Planning where the deceased worked sent
his death gratuity amounting to Kshs. 43,817.90 in 1984 to the Department
of Administrator General. The same was handed to the Administrators
of the deceased's estate in 1997, by then the total had risen to Kshs.
80,556.95 due to the interest earned.

As of now, the Administrator General is holding close to over a million
Kenya shillings which amount did not form part of the deceased's estate;
This is from Civil Servants' Group Accident Claim (CSGA) sent to us
for our distribution to the dependants. The principal sum having been
Kshs. 251,400. Today the total stands at Kshs.1,005,261.60 because
of interest from 1984.

The Administrator-General has not been able to dispose off this amount
in accordance with the Law, because the dependants have not been established
conclusively.

From your letter you state that you are the deceased's son, kindly would
you tell me how many brothers and sisters you have out there and the
relationship between your mother and the deceased.

- 2 -

According to information held by me, the following is the list of dependants who stand to benefit from the above claim:-

1. Abongo Malik Obama
2. Rital Auma Obama   son
3. Mark Okoth Obama   daughter
4. David Opiyo Obama   son
5. Barry Obama Jnr.   son
6. Jael Atieno Obama   son
7. George Hussein Obama   widow

                    son

I will be grateful to get an earlier response from you.

Yours faithfully,

MRS. MUKULU KARIUKI
SENIOR PRINCIPAL STATE COUNSEL
FOR PUBLIC TRUSTEE

NB: As to the size of the deceased's estate, its only the administrators of the estate who could supply the answer.

/ewm

A F F I D A V I T.

I, Asha Akumu Orinda - ID/1528551/64, do hereby declare and confirm that:-

(a) I was born at Karabondi sub-location, Kokela village, East Karachuonyo location in South Nyanza and my father's name is Njoga s/- Okela of Karabondi, Karachuonyo.

(b) That, currently I live in Kowuor Sub-location, Ongang village, South Karachuonyo (Kanyaluo) in South Nyanza.

(c) That, I was first married in East Alego, Kogelo, Nyangoma where I stayed for several years and broke the marriage later and got remarried at Wagwe, Karachuonyo, South Nyanza and reside at the moment at the place indicated at No. (b) above.

(d) That, my first husband was the late Onyango Hussein s/o Obama of Alego and second husband is Mr. Salmin Orinda of Karachuonyo as indicated at No. (c) above.

(e) That, I am the real mother of the late Dr. Hussein Barack Obama who passed away on 26th November, 1982.

(f) That, at the time I was married to the late Onyango Hussein of Alego, I gave birth to five children namel; Sara Nyaoke, Dr. Hussein Barack Obama, Mwunahawa -una, Rashid Ndalo and Adhil Pwata.

(g) That, Dr. Hussein Barack Obama was my second child and that, of my five children with the late Onyango Hussein only two of them namely; Sara Nyaoke and Mwenahawa Auma are still alive.

(h) That, to my actual knowledge, my late son Dr. Hussein Barack Obama was first married to Mrs. Grace Kezia Aoko with whom they stayed and gave birth to the first two children only prior to her divorce from the late Obama. The divorce was customarily just as was the case with their marriage with the deceased.

(i) That, Mrs. Kezia Aoko divorced the late Obama in 1964 and to the best of my knowledge, she stayed away upto and until the time when the late Dr. Obama met his death. She only attended
the funeral of the late

123

..... 2 .....

(j) That, Dr. Obama married also to two European ladies one after another and also divorced subsequently. The first lady was the second wife while the other one was the third wife to the deceased. The second European wife to the deceased gave birth to one male child while the third wife gave birth to two male children to the deceased.

(k) That, the second and third wifes (Europeans) also divorced Dr. Obama subsequently after giving birth to the deceased as per No. (j) above.

(l) That, the late Dr. Obama got married to the forth wife Mrs. Jael Atieno Obama in 1981 and Mrs. Atieno lived with the deceased as wife and husband upto and until the time of his death. Prior to the death of her late husband, she gave birth to one male child to the deceased and has not at any time deserted the home of her late husband, the late Dr. Obama.

(m) That, I as mother of the deceased opted to make this affidavit because there have been alot of conflicting informations given to Government particularly by the first wife Mrs. Grace Kezia and hope that these clarifications will have to solve whatsever might have been unclear as far as the deceased's marriage and the positions of the marriage thereafter are concerned. I used to meet my late son and discussed various issues including his marital affairs. I am therefore clearly nowledgable of many of his afairs including his marital issues.

SWORN BEFORE ME THIS MONDAY 20TH AUGUST OF THE CALENDER YEAR, 1 9 8 4

RESIDENT MAGISTRATE S I A Y A.

R E S I D E N T.

REPUBLIC OF KENYA

IN THE HIGH COURT OF KENYA AT NAIROBI

SUCCESSION CAUSE NO. 233 OF 1985

IN THE MATTER OF THE ESTATE OF BARRACK HUSSEIN OBAMA - (DECEASED)

A N D

IN THE MATTER OF APPLICATION FOR LETTERS OF ADMINISTRATION

- BY -

GRACE KEZIA AOKO :::APPLICANT
AND
JAEL ATIENO OBAMA :::OBJECTOR

AFFIDAVIT

I, JAEL ATIENO OBAMA of the Ministry of Planning and National Development, The Treasury, P.O. Box 30007, Nairobi in the Republic of Kenya hereby make Oath and state as follows:-

1. That I am the Objector in this suit and as such I am duly authorised to swear this Affidavit.

2. That I have perused the record herein and the purported Application for Grant of Letters of Administration by GRACE KEZIA AOKO and I wish to state as hereunder.

3. That I am the sole surviving and legal widow of the late Barrack Hussein Obama, Deceased.

4. That I was lawfully married to the Deceased on the 12th day of April 1981 in Nairobi under Luo Customary Law and the Objector stayed with the Deceased in the matrimonial home and cohabited with the Deceased as husband and wife until the Deceased died.

5. That I gave birth to a son naturally fathered by and a product of the deceased at Nairobi on the 7th day of May 1982, namely GEORGE HUSSEIN ONYANGO.

6. That I and my said son are entitled to be the sole beneficiaries to the Estate of the Deceased.

7. That the Applicant herein, GRACE KEZIA AOKO had been lawfully divorced from the Deceased under Luo Customary Law.

8. That after the said legal divorce of the Applicant by the Deceased, the Applicant got re-married to another husband and had two...

- 2 -

9. That after the said divorce and re-marriage by the Applicant, to the best of my information and belief, the Applicant was never re-united to the Deceased and never visited him or lived together with him, the Deceased, since 1965.

10. That the Applicant and her children Samson and Bernard or any of her other children are not entitled in law to inherit any of the Deceased's property and are definitely not entitled to Grant of Letters of Administration in the Estate. Annexed hereto and marked "JAO" is a letter dated 19-1-84 from the Public Trustee.

11. That the Applicant has falsely and maliciously mislead others that the Deceased's mother is dead, or is not available.

12. That the truth is that the lawful and natural mother of the Deceased, namely, MRS. ASHA AKUMU ORINDA (ID/NO. 1528551/64) is alive and available and is ready to participate in the Estate of her deceased son.

13. That my child, George Hussein Onyango's copy of Birth Certificate is annexed hereto and marked "JAO 2".

14. That I have referred the matter of the Administration of my Deceased Estate to the Public Trustee and the Cause is recorded with the Public Trustee as Administration Cause No. 310 of 1983.

15. That consequently it is fair and Just that the Public Trustee be alerted of this Application and be joined as a party hereto.

16. That it will be fair and just that before Letters of Administration are granted to me or to any other person or persons whether jointly or severally, that formal evidence be taken and parties be cross-examined and Documents scrutinised and appropriate witnesses called to testify to enable the Court to arrive at a just decision.

17. That also annexed hereto and marked "JAO 3" is a photostat copy of an Affidavit.

18. That annexed hereto and marked "JAO 4" is a photostat copy of my Pay slip showing my name.

19. That the temporary or interim Grant to the Applicant should not only be restricted or suspended, but should be revoked and cancelled and a proper grant made in my name and my son George Hussein Onyango.

20. That I make this Affidavit in support of my Objection and Application that I be granted Leave to file my formal Answer and formal Application

- 3 -

under Rule 17 (5) by way of CROSS PETITION for the grant to me
of Letters of Administration exclusively in the Estate of the Deceased.
That the facts deponed to herein are true to the best of my knowledge
information and belief.

AND I amake this Solemn Affidavit conscientiously believing the same
to be true and in accordance with the Oaths and Statutory Declarations
Act.

by the said JAEL   )
ENO OBAMA at Nairobi this   )
25th day of Nov. 1986.   )
)
BEFORE   ME   )
)
)   ....(signature)...........
)   (Jael   Atieno Obama)
)
)
COMMISSIONER FOR OATHS.   )

Bibliography

Aseka, Erick (1993). *Ronald Ngala*. Nairobi: East African Educational Publishers.

Ayot, T Olunga, (1987). *The Luo Settlement in South Nyanza*. Nairobi: Educational Research and Publication Ltd.

Borchert, Peter. *Africa Geographic*, February 2011 issue. Cape Town: Africa Geographic (Pty) Ltd.

Bhutto, Benazir (1989). *Daughter of Destiny: An Autobiography*. New York: Simon & Schuster.

Cohen, William and E S Atieno Odhiambo (2004). *The Risks of Knowledge: Investigations into the Death of the Hon Minister John Robert Ouko in Kenya*. Athens: Ohio University Press.

Diop, Cheik Anta, (Translated from the French by Mercer Cook, 1974). *The African Origin of Civilisation: Myth or reality*, New York: Lawrence Hill and Company.

Dougherty, Steve & Buell, Hal (2009). *Hopes and Dreams: The Story of Barack Obama*. New York: Black Dog Leventhal.

Fedders, Andrew and Cynthia Salvadon (1979). *Peoples and Cultures of Kenya*. Nairobi: TransAfrica/Rex Collings.

Goldsworthy, David (1982). *Tom Mboya: The Man Kenya Wanted to Forget*. Nairobi: East African Educational Publishers.

Hartley, Jean (2005). *This is Kenya*. London: New Holland Publishing.

Jacobs, Sally (2011). *The Other Barack: The Bold and Reckless Life of President Obama's Father*. New York: Public Affairs.

Karume, Njenga (2009). *Beyond Expectations: From Charcoal to Gold (An Autobiography)*. Nairobi: East African Educational Publishers.

LeAnne, Shel (2009). *Say it like Obama*. New York: McGraw-Hill.

Mboya, Paul (1997). *Luo, Kitgi gi Timbegi (A Handbook of Luo Customs)*. Nairobi: Self published.

Mboya, Tom (1986). *Freedom and After*. Nairobi: East African Educational Publishers.

Ndegwa, Duncan (2007). *Walking in Kenyatta's Struggles*. Nairobi: Kenya Leadership Institute.

Ng'ang'a, Wanguhu (2006). *Kenya's Ethnic Communities: Foundation of the Nation*. Nairobi: Gatundu Publishers Ltd.

Obama, Barack (2004). *Dreams from My Father*. New York: Three Rivers Press.

_____ (2006). *The Audacity of Hope: Thoughts on Reclaiming the American Dream*. New York: Three Rivers Press.

Obama, George with Damien Lewis (2010). *Homeland*. New York: Simon &Schuster.

Ogot, Bethwell (2009). *A History of the Luo-Speaking Peoples of Eastern Africa*. Kisumu: Anyange Press.

_____ (2004). *A Political and Cultural History of the Jii-SpeakingPeoples of Eastern Africa*. Kisumu: Anyange Press.

_____ (2003). *My footprints on the Sands of Time*. Kisumu: Anyange Press.

Ogot, Grace (1990). *The Promised Land*. Nairobi: East African Educational Publishers.

Poitier, Sidney (2008). *Life Beyond Measure*. New York: Simon & Schuster.

_____ (2000). *The Measure of a Man: A Memoir*. New York: Simon & Schuster.

Schachtman, Tom (2009). *Airlift to America*. New York: St Martins Press.

Wachira, Kondia Mwaniki (2008). *Kenya Book of Records*. Nairobi: Africa Books of Records Enterprises.

Wandibba, Simiyu (1996). *Masinde Muliro*. Nairobi: East Africa Educational Publishers.

Wilson, Gordon (1961). Chik gi Tim Luo. Nairobi: Government Printer.

_____ (1968). *Luo Customary Law and Marriage Customs*. Nairobi: Government Printer.

Index